A PIMA REMEMBERS

by

GEORGE WEBB

UNIVERSITY OF ARIZONA PRESS

TUCSON

COPYRIGHT 1959 BY GEORGE WEBB

FOREWORD

GEORGE WEBB was born about 1893 at Gila Crossing on the Gila River Reservation, some twenty miles south of Phoenix, Arizona. His father was struggling with the problems of farming along the river at a time when white men upstream were appropriating nearly all the water. His parents wanted him to have as much schooling as possible. They sent him, at the age of six, to the Gila Crossing Day School. He attended for a year and then went on to the Indian Bureau Boarding School in 1902. He spent ten years there, graduating in 1912. From 1914 to 1917 he attended public high school in Phoenix, when that school had an enrollment of 800. He left high school in 1917 and went to work for a year as a ranch-hand near Glendale, Arizona, until he was appointed by the Indian Agent at Sacaton as a farm overseer at Gila Crossing. He served in this capacity for three years, managing farm operations, and at some time during this period enrolled in the Cook Bible Institute.

When George Webb was twenty-eight he bought cattle of his own and married Hattie MacDonald of his own village of Gila Crossing. For the next twenty-seven years he raised cattle and farmed intermittently when there was sufficient irrigation water. He and Mrs. Webb raised a family of seven children, four boys and three girls. Two of the boys served in the United States Armed

Forces, one in Europe and another in Korea. In 1934 George Webb was elected representative from Gila Crossing to the first Tribal Council. In 1938 he gave up trying to farm because of shortage of water and ran a grocery store for two years.

In 1940 the Webbs moved near Chandler, and in 1948 sold out their cattle. For the past nine years George Webb has lived as a retired cattleman on his farm. In 1942 he was appointed Associate Judge of the Tribal Court and served until 1950. After his retirement he conceived the idea of writing these sketches of Pima history and traditions.

His narrative is aimed at two audiences. On the one hand, it was inspired by his desire to acquaint younger Pimas with some of the background and traditions of their people; traditions in the process of being forgotten. He also wanted to reach white men who misunderstand the position of Pimas in modern American life. For both audiences Mr. Webb seasons his story with genial, but often deep-cutting humor.

Edward H. Spicer
University of Arizona

PREFACE

THIS book is written with the young Pima Indians in mind. Very few Pima parents tell their children about the customs and habits of their forefathers. Therefore the present young Pimas do not know of the early life of their people.

With my own forefathers as informants I write this narration which is part of the lives they went through.

You will notice that I give no dates as my informants gave none, only the order of events as put down in this writing.

When I was young, the old Pimas could remember a long way back in time. They did not have any writing, but they did have what is called a Calendar Stick. On this stick they carved signs that reminded them of things they wanted to remember. Sometimes in the evenings they would look at this stick and tell what had happened in their grandfathers' time. Or they would remember a story.

These forefathers of mine never had any of the whiteman's education. They were educated in the ways of nature and used natural resources for food and clothing. This may have something to do with their long lives as they lived to be very old.

This writing is done in a very simple way so that the Indian with the least education may read and understand it. I did not try to go into the origin of the Pimas more than to tell a few legends that may throw some light on where they came from. Stories were handed down from generation to generation, but today there are only a few of us who know them, and we do not make a practice of telling them. The whole story of White Clay Eater takes four nights to tell so I did not attempt to tell it all, only a short part.

When I finished writing this book I did not know how to go about getting it published.

I called up the Tucson Indian School and they sent Miss Audrey Bard, English teacher, to go over the writing. She introduced me to the Chairman of the Folk-lore Committee at the University of Arizona, Miss Frances Gillmor, who placed this writing in the hands of Dr. E. H. Spicer of the Anthropology Department. Dr. Spicer arranged for Mr. Harry Behn to design the book and prepare it for publication by the University.

I want to thank Mrs. Harry Childson of Apache Junction also for her help and Mr. Dean Saxton for his assistance with the proper way of writing the Pima words.

I am thankful to meet such good people.

George Webb

CONTENTS

A PEACEFUL LIFE 11

THE BATTLE OF AJI 22

A RABBIT HUNT 26

THE OLD WAYS 29

THE FIRST WHITE MEN 34

EARLY DAYS 38

PIMA GAMES 42

THE APACHE WARS 45

PROGRESS 49

THOSE WHO ARE GONE 53

BOYHOOD 57

SCHOOL DAYS 61

THE GREAT WHEAT HARVEST 64

FLOOD 69

THE PIMA LANGUAGE 71

HORSE ROUND-UP 76

THE MISSION 84

PIMA LEGENDS 90

LEGEND OF THE HUHUGAM 92

THE LEGEND OF HO'OK 95

EAGLEMAN 99

LEGEND OF THE GREAT FLOOD 104

LEGEND OF THE BIG DROUGHT 106

WHITE CLAY EATER 109

THE LEGEND OF TODAY 116

LAND 119

WATER 121

SOME PEOPLE MENTIONED IN THIS WRITING

Buzzing Feather
Juana Losso
Eaglefeathers
Swift Arrow
Grayhorse
Keli·hi
Rainbow's Ends

A FEW PIMA WORDS

amog   a speech
vato   shade
olas-ki   old Pima round house
Jujkam   Mexicans
Miliga·n   white people
chu'i   pinole candy
ato-'ova'igo   Pima war cry
ban-vivega   coyote tobacco
vi-hog   mesquite beans
wulivega   arrow target
ku·sheda   rabbit hunt on horseback
shaa-tha   rabbit hunt on foot

A PEACEFUL LIFE

WAY out in the southwestern part of our country which is now the State of Arizona, there was a Pima Indian Village.

It was a day in the early part of spring. The desert was covered with green grass and the trees were just beginning to put forth their leaves. The sun had been shining brightly and was now low over the horizon.

Juana Losso stood on a little knoll not far from her brush home. With hand shading her eyes she was looking towards the distant hills watching for a glimpse of dust that would tell the return of her husband Eagle-feathers from a hunting trip. Beside her was a little boy of two summers whose name was Keli•hi, which means "Old Fashioned."

Not seeing any dust Juana Losso and her little boy walked slowly back toward their home.

Just then two other boys came running over the desert. They were also sons of Juana Losso, and older than little Keli•hi. With them was a dog.

Grayhorse had a cottontail rabbit hanging from a cotton string tied around his waist. Swift Arrow had two quail hanging from his cotton string belt.

This cotton string belt the boys wore held up their gee-strings, the only clothing the Pimas wore in those days. Juana Losso wore the usual dress of the women which was a cotton cloth wrapped around her waist hanging down to the knees.

The boys and their mother were all barefooted, although sometimes they wore sandals made from cow or horse hide.

Grayhorse and Swift Arrow were both talking at the same time trying to tell their mother how they had killed the rabbit and the two quail.

She listened. Then with a little laughter she took the rabbit and the quail to clean.

After she had cleaned them, she sharpened the ends of a stick and stuck it through the rabbit lengthwise. With the quail she did the same and put them up to the fire to cook.

While the rabbit and the quail were cooking, Juana Losso went to the storage-basket and took out some *vi-hog* (mesquite beans) and pounded them into a powder on the *chu-pa* (mortar). This powder was mixed with water and used as a sweet drink.

Sometimes the powder is put into a clay bowl, sprinkled with water, and covered with a damp cloth to harden into a cake when dry. This cake is put away and kept in store for winter. Eating a small piece of this cake, a Pima could go all day without other food.

The cooking of the quail and rabbit was now done, so Juana Losso with her three boys, Grayhorse, Swift Arrow and little Keli·hi, and their dog Tua-chin-kam sat around the fire to eat.

The dog suddenly sat up and looked out into the darkness.

They all stopped eating and Grayhorse and Swift Arrow jumped up and ran to meet their father who had come home with a deer.

After Eaglefeathers unsaddled his horse and hobbled it out, they all went back to the fire. Grayhorse and Swift Arrow were both trying to tell their father how they killed the quail and rabbit. Grayhorse was telling how Tua-chinkam chased the rabbit into a bush, keeping it there by barking while he shot an arrow and killed it.

Swift Arrow was telling how Tua-chinkam scared up the quail and how they flew into a tree and sat there while the dog kept barking at them.

"The quail just sat there while I picked out my best arrows and shot them, two of them with only two arrows!" said Swift Arrow.

The boys patted the dog who had helped them.

In those days Pima boys learned to use the bow and arrow when they were very young. That is how they became experts when they grew older.

The boys hunted separately from the older men. Their game consisted of small birds, such as doves and quail, and also cotton tail rabbit.

They did not make their own bow and arrows. A grandpa or an uncle always made them, of a size fitting the size of the boy.

The little Pima boys are proud to carry a bow and arrows made by Grandpa. They learn to use it by shooting at a target, called *wulivega,* which is a small bundle of grass wrapped with willow or mesquite bark about six inches long and two inches around. The boys throw the target ahead ten to twenty feet, each boy taking his turn in shooting one arrow at it.

Juana Losso now began to cook a piece of the deer meat for her husband.

Her cooking place was a round shelter of arrow-weeds stuck in the ground, held in place by a few willow or mesquite posts. The fire was built in the center, with clay pots and ollas of water and food around it. Most always this enclosure was under a mesquite tree.

The Pimas in those days seldom ate a noon meal, only a little cactus syrup with whole wheat bread or *chu'i* in the early afternoon. The evening meal was eaten whenever the men came home from the day's hunting or work in the fields.

They cooked the meat by holding it over the open fire or placing it on the live coals, at other times burying it in the hot ashes.

Here I shall tell how a Pima cooks rabbit in the ashes:

First you dig a trench in the ground, a little bigger than the rabbit. Build a good sized fire in and over the trench. Then clean the rabbit in this way, leaving the skin on: cut the stomach open just enough to

14

take the intestines out, but leave the heart, liver and as much of the blood as you can. After getting the stomach cleaned out, take a small green stick, sharpen one end and use this as a pin to close the cut.

By this time the fire has burned down leaving hot coals. Now take a long green stick and push the coals out of the trench leaving a few at the bottom. Then place the rabbit in the hot trench, bottom side up, and cover over with hot ashes and coals. Rebuild the fire on top and let it cook for about forty minutes or more as depends on the heat of your fire. When the fire dies down, take your long stick again and take the rabbit out. The skin will pick right off. Then eat! You will find that a rabbit cooked in this manner tastes very good. Especially when you are hungry.

A *vato* or shade was usually just a few yards from this cooking place. This shelter of a type still used by the Pimas was made with four or six upright forked posts that held cross-poles on which arrow weeds were placed to make the shade. This shelter was open on all sides and was used in the summer time when the sun shines hot. There was always a large olla full of drinking water in the center of the *vato*. On a small rope stretched between the poles, strings of dried meat were hanging, or a small olla full of *chu'i* or pinole.

A double rope tied loosely and covered with a cotton cloth made a swing for the baby. Juana Losso

often put little Keli•hi in this swing and as she swung
the ropes back and forth she sang:

> Ululu 'ululu 'ululu' u
> My little baby is going to sleep,
> For I am standing here swinging you,
> As I am a little cricket,
> As I am a little cricket.

With the singing of this song, the baby soon went
to sleep and Juana Losso was free to go about her work.

Beyond the *vato* was the *olas-ki,* or round-house,
made of mesquite posts, willow and arrow weeds. This
type of house is no longer used. It was enclosed all
around, with a little dirt and straw on top to keep the
rain out. The only opening was a small hole about two
feet wide and four feet high which was used as a door.
This door was always to the east. To get in, one had to
get down on hands and knees.

You may wonder what the Pimas did for ventilation in such a house. That was very simple. The sides
were covered with only arrow weeds. There was plenty
of fresh air. Fire was seldom built in the *olas-ki* but in
the winter a scoop-full of red hot coals was brought in
and placed in the center on the dirt floor.

Around the four center posts, next to the wall
there were sleeping mats made from yucca leaves. On
these mats were home-made blankets woven from cotton. The Pimas grew their own cotton which they wove
into cloth and blankets. The *olas-ki* was used only in

rainy or cold weather. At all other times the open *vato* was the center of the home.

The Pimas are out-of-doors people and stay out in the open most of the time.

Up to the time I am remembering there had been no white people in our part of the country, except some Spanish explorers who passed through but never stayed. At this time though, the Pimas had heard of many white people over towards the east, but none had come out this far.

So the Pimas were enjoying a free and primitive life, living from day to day not knowing Sunday from any other day. But they knew their seasons and planted their crops accordingly and they prospered.

The Pima Indians have farmed along the Gila river for many, many years. Although we have no record, except the primitive Calendar Stick, it was told from one generation to the other that the Pima Indians have always lived along the Gila river.

The seeds were also handed down from generation to generation, and where they first got them, I do not know. They planted corn, a soft corn now known as Indian corn, and beans white and yellow, and squash, melons, wheat, tobacco and cotton. The tobacco they grew was called *ban-vivega* (coyote tobacco). Only a few tobacco plants were grown by elderly Pimas as only the old people and the medicine-man smoked.

Their implements were crude. Such as the wooden

plow, wooden shovel and planting stick. A pitch fork was made by cutting a long forked limb from a mesquite tree. After the branches were cut away, there was a pitch fork with a long handle.

A wooden plow was made from a good-sized mesquite tree. Only certain Pimas knew how to make the wooden plow and they made all plows used. These wooden plows were drawn by oxen. The ox came from cattle left by the early Spaniards. Also the horse. The horse was not used for heavy work but only for riding on long trips. In those days the Pimas travelled even as far as Hermosillo in Sonora, Mexico. They also went to a certain spot to gather cactus fruit and mesquite beans in season. Some went as far east as what is now known as Picacho. These Pimas knew all the water holes in the desert.

In the spring of the year at a certain moon they went out to their fields to plant. These fields were small but the yield was always good. The low bottom land along the Gila River was very fertile, made so by the over-flow of the flood-water.

Early in the morning of each day a man would stand on top of a *vato* making a speech which went something like this:

> Now another day is coming,
> Awake from slumber,
> Look toward the east,
> See the rising of the sun,

Which means another day to toil.
Another day to hunt for meat,
To put the seed in the ground
That the yield might be good,
So our people may not go hungry.
The great Father provided us the sun
To give life to our earth so
That it might give us a good yield.
And that we might see
To hunt our game for meat.
So arise and make use of the day
And do not get in the way
Of the women as they go about
Fixing up the camp and the
Needed task of preparing meals for you.
Many moons, many suns have come and gone
Since our forefathers here on this same ground
Toiled and struggled so that we might
Enjoy life today.
So let us not waste this day.
But get your tools, go out to the field, or
Take down your bow and arrows
And go after the game, so that
Your family will not be in need of meat.
So now I hope you will strive
To make this day the best in your life.

This speech was usually made just before sun-up
by a man with a clear voice and could be heard a mile
away. The man spoke about five minutes and when he
finished talking the Village suddenly became alive. The
young boys started out to find the horses or oxen, while

19

the girls went after water, sometimes going for miles before they found the stock or water. The young boys knew the track of their animals and followed it until they found them.

The women started the fire to cook the morning meal to have it ready by the time the children got back with the stock. The men took the seed out and carried it down to the field.

After breakfast, everybody went to the field to plant, with the exception of a few women and children who stayed home to prepare a little something to eat and take it down to the field in the early afternoon. The whole village went out to plant and stayed out until sun down.

The wheat that was planted in the fall was just turning yellow and in another moon would be ready to harvest. The heads of the wheat were plucked by hand and put into a cloth, carried over the shoulder, forming a sack on the side. When the sack was full, the ends were tied together, put on top of the head and carried to a place cleared and leveled for the threshing.

After they had cleared the field of grain, the men took long sticks and beat the seed out. After the seed was threshed out, the women took large round baskets, filled them with the threshed grain, held them up in the air, shaking them enough to let the grain fall a little at a time so the wind could blow the chaff away. After the grain was cleaned, it was taken to the storage baskets.

The storage baskets where Eaglefeathers stored

his grain were made of arrow-weeds and bark, about four foot deep, six foot wide and were set up on a platform off the ground. The Pimas call this platform a *homta*. Sometimes a group of these *homomta* could be seen near the *vato* or *ki*. A few can still be seen.

THE BATTLE OF AJI

EAGLEFEATHERS lived about a mile east and a little south of what is now known as Pima Butte. The Pimas called it Aji. The people of Aji at first were not Pimas. They were known as the Hiat-ab-o'otam, meaning "people of the sand dunes," as they lived on little sand dunes. They were part of a group of Papagos who came to the Gila River from the south and settled there. They married and were adopted into the Pima tribe. They finally settled down at a place called Santa Cruz Village. Today that village is called Hya-thob.

Across the Gila River, due north of Pima Butte, lived another tribe of Indians, known by the Pimas as O'obab or Maricopas. These O'obab were said to have been at one time a part of the Yuma tribe. For some reason they had some sort of disagreement and became separated from the Yumas and came up the Gila River. Finding the Pimas friendly they settled near them.

One day a group of Yuma warriors followed these O'obab and made a raid on their village. The O'obab being only a few in number were unable to hold off the Yumas. So a messenger was sent to the nearest Pima Village for help.

Eaglefeathers' village, being the closest, received the message. He immediately sent another messenger to the next Pima Village. That Pima Village on receiving the message, did the same and the next and the next until all the villages up the Gila River were notified.

Eaglefeathers put on his war-paint and ordered the boys to bring his best horse. He took down his fighting bow and arrows, tightened the string on the bow, looked down the length of the arrows to see if they were straight so that they might fly true. Putting the arrows back into the container he swung it to his back and went out to his horse. He rode over to Pima Butte where already a number of Pima warriors were gathered.

Looking east up the Gila River, he saw clouds of dust as warriors from the other villages, receiving the message about the Yumas, were coming to help their good friends the O'obab. Clouds of dust could be seen as far east as Sacaton, eighteen miles away, for some of the warriors were coming from Blackwater, ten miles farther east.

In looking toward the north from Pima Butte, Eaglefeathers could see smoke rising as the Yuma warriors set fire to the brush houses of the O'obab.

When the Pimas had gathered sufficient men, they moved across the river to attack the raiding Yumas.

The Yumas, seeing the Pimas come across the river, lined up to fight.

When the Pimas got there, they too lined up. But before the actual battle took place, each side made a challenge to a certain warrior of whom they had heard to meet in the center and fight.

One of the Yumas would say:

"Lone Arrow!

I, Chief Many Horses, have heard of your deeds!

Come forth, that my people may see if your greatness is what you say it is!"

The two would meet in the center for combat. When one overcame the other, another couple would make a challenge and meet in the same manner.

This went on until one of the Pimas gave the battle cry, *"ato'ova'igo!"* Then all the Pima warriors went forward and chased the Yumas toward the Estrella Mountains, killing as they chased.

These Yumas got within two miles of the Estrella Mountains when the Pimas closed in on them, killing the few remaining Yumas.

This happened about sun-down. One of the Yumas, left for dead during the fight, came to in the darkness with only the stars shining.

He got up and looked around. Seeing his companions lying dead, he said:

"If any of you are, as I am, alive, get up and let us start for home!"

No one answered, so he made his way to his home —two hundred miles away — to tell his people what had happened.

Little Keli·hi was about six winters old when these Yumas came. The day after the fight, he and some of the boys from Eaglefeathers' village went over to

24

where the fighting took place. They saw the Yuma dead still lying where they fell.

The weapons used by the Pima warriors in this fight were the bow and arrows, the war club and shield. The bow and arrows were used in distant fighting and the war club and shield in close combat.

The Yumas used knives and lances. A few used bow and arrows.

In those days, a Pima warrior coming toward you holding one of those shields in front of him, jigging, side-stepping, watching every move you made from over the edge of the shield, was considered very dangerous. If you shot an arrow at him he merely side-stepped, holding the shield at an angle in the path of the arrow. When it hit the shield, it only glanced off to one side. And before you were ready for a second shot, the warrior was upon you knocking the weapon out of your hand and putting his war club into effective use. A Pima warrior with those weapons was a man to look out for.

After the fighting was over, everyone was quiet and peaceful again. The Pimas went about their harvesting and storing food for the coming winter.

The O'obab went to rebuilding their arrow-weed homes destroyed by the Yumas.

Had it not been for the support of the Pimas, this small band of Indians would have been wiped out entirely as they were greatly out-numbered by the Yumas.

A RABBIT HUNT

WHEN the Pimas were not working in their fields, they would often go on a rabbit hunt on horse back, which they called *ku·sheda*.

Early in the morning you would hear a man making an *amog* (speech) from the top of a *vato* telling the people of the coming day's hunt. He would name a certain place to meet before they would start hunting.

After a number of men got together at the place designated they would start their hunt. They would follow a certain route until a rabbit was scared up, and the chase was on till they ran down and killed that one rabbit. Then they would all gather together, talking and laughing about the happenings on the chase. How a horse stepped in a badger hole and fell, throwing the rider, breaking his arrows. If all his arrows were broken, the other hunters would each give him one to use.

Then they would go on to find another rabbit. Game was plentiful in those days and each hunter usually killed one or more rabbits.

Once in a while someone did not kill any. Then someone who had killed more than one, would give him a rabbit. In this way no one came home empty handed.

If you could have seen the skill and marksmanship on these hunts, you would be amazed. Imagine a horse running at full speed! The rider draws on his bow, sending an arrow to its mark, while the rabbit with ears flat is running as fast as it can!

Sometimes the rabbit was not hit enough to fall and could still run with the arrow sticking in him. The hunters would begin yelling, "jeva! jeva!" meaning, "rotten, rotten!" The next person who put an arrow into the rabbit and felled it could claim it.

Sometimes two arrows hit one rabbit at about the same time. Then the first of the two boys whose arrows hit the rabbit could put a second arrow into the rabbit, and claim it. These rules were generally understood by all and nobody ever disputed them.

In those days the desert was always covered with grass and the stock was in good condition. A horse was always in good running shape. The hunt kept them so.

Sometimes the Pimas went hunting on foot which they call *shaa-tha.* On these hunts on foot, they would kill cotton tail rabbits, doves and quail. A Pima is a good runner. You should see him hunting quail. A quail only flies a short way. When it flies, the Pima is running under it. When it lands he is right there to kill it. Even old men.

THE OLD WAYS

A PIMA Indian worked and lived outside most of the time. He was seldom sick. Many lived to be over a hundred years old. The old people were looked upon with much respect by the young people for sound advice and good counsel. Sickness or diseases were unknown until after the coming of the white man.

Little Keli·hi always looked up to the old people. That's why he was called Keli·hi, as the name means "Old Fashioned" in the Pima language. He was always to be found among the older people. This way of early life enabled him to become one of the leaders of his people, as we will find later in this story.

These Pimas were governed by certain head men who made rules for the villagers and these villagers lived accordingly. No one knows how long they lived in this manner, but when the Spaniards found them, these humble and prosperous farming people were living by the law of the common good.

Their children grew up and married someone from another village, because a whole village was related. The young people married whenever their parents found a good mate. Divorces were unheard of. It was the custom of a young Pima man, when he married a young lady, to take her to live with his parents. Never with her parents. Whenever a boy brought a girl home there was much excitement, sometimes so much excitement that the boy's parents did things they never intended to do. Always they gave gifts of wheat or beans to the girl's parents. But sometimes they got so excited they gave a horse or a cow.

The Pima Indians always had plenty. They planted crops and owned stock. But the poor Apaches who lived in the mountains to the north did not do any farming and so once in a while they would come down and raid the Pimas.

Sometimes the Apaches found the Pimas in resistance and had to kill a few of them to get their supply of food. Then the Pimas would follow the Apaches to their camp. In the fight the Pimas would kill as many Apaches as they could, leaving the women and children. Among the Pimas, it was always a dishonor to kill a woman or child. Sometimes, rather than leave the women and children orphaned, the Pima warriors would bring home an Apache woman or child.

We have now among our tribe Pimas who have Apache ancestors, descendants of people in that period. In my family, one of my uncles married an Apache woman brought home in those days, and I have Pima-Apache cousins living today. But no Pima warrior was allowed to take any Apache woman or child home unless he was capable of giving them a decent home. So most of the time after a battle they would leave them and not bother to bring them home.

On one of these trips a Pima warrior brought home an Apache boy, whom he called Hejel-wi'ikam, in the Pima language meaning "Left Alone." This little Apache boy was treated as his own son.

Some white people passing through the Pima village saw the little boy playing. They knew that he was Apache. They took a liking to the boy and asked if they could take him along. The Pima said No! And so the white people promised to give the boy a good home and education.

After much consideration, the old Pima warrior finally agreed to let this little Apache boy go. This boy later became a noted man, the famous Doctor Montezuma, a great surgeon.

Some time ago I happened to be at Fort McDowell and one of the boys told me that the Doctor was there and very sick. He asked me if I would like to see him. I said I would like to see him very much.

He took me to an *olas-ki* made of willow poles and brush covered with a canvas. There was a passage way about four feet high, three feet wide and about three yards long. To get in, I had to get down on my hands and knees. There, on the dirt floor, was spread an expensive blanket on which the Doctor lay. To one side was a suitcase full of expensive clothes. The room was full of people. My visit was very brief as the Doctor was on his last stage of life.

A few days later he died.

In those days the old Pimas could often tell what was going to happen by seeing it in a dream.

Even white people came to believe this.

One night one of the Pimas had a dream. He dreamed that the Apaches came and made a raid on the Pima village. This warrior held a meeting of the other men and told them of his dream.

Some of the warriors said:

"It might be true!"

So, early the next day they went out to scout the nearby hills. They went out and just before they got to the hills, they met the Apaches, who were also scouting for a way to attack the village.

When they saw the Pimas, they ran back toward the hills with the Pimas after them.

One Apache had already started to climb the hill when he turned around and came down toward the Pimas so fast he could not stop himself.

The first Pima, in order to avoid a collision, jumped to one side, but in doing so, his heel caught in the leg of his pants made with wide open bottoms similar to a Navy boy's pants.

The Apache came to a stop, drew on his bow, sending an arrow aimed at the heart of the Pima.

The Pima twisted to one side in time to have the arrow miss its mark. But it did pierce the skin on his breast, going through the arm and pinning the arm to his side. The Pima jumped up and with one hand scuffled with the Apache until other Pimas came up to help him. He was saved.

One of the Pima scouting party was sent back to Eaglefeathers' village to tell the news. This scout ran all the way, a distance of about eight miles.

The spot where the Pimas and Apaches fought is now marked with good sized rocks, near the hills south of what is now the town of Maricopa.

Keli•hi was about twelve winters old when this happened. He and most of the villagers rode out on horse-back to see the dead Apache.

The Pimas had a custom in those days, if any warrior killed an enemy, he had to fast for four days. During those four days the medicine-man was very busy shaking the rattle, drawing buzzard feathers back and forth over the hero's body and blowing tobacco smoke and singing to drive the evil spirits away.

This is the song he would sing:

You have killed your enemy.
As I toss you away, you see
Birds with flapping wings.
Between those wings
You must pass to the west.

I bind your hair,
I twist it tight in a rough knot,
I bind your hair
And pin it with a sharp stick.

THE FIRST WHITE MEN

The Pimas are peaceful people but also good warriors. They will fight whenever necessary to protect their property and rights. They also have been known to fight for their fellow-beings as they did for the O'obab in the battle of Aji. But never against the white man.

Eaglefeathers saw the first white men come into the Pima country.

One day during a hot summer some strange people came to his camp. Their skins were white and they had over their bodies strange garments. They wore leather from their knees to their feet. Some were walking while others rode in long boxes on wheels. These boxes were covered with canvas and drawn by oxen. Little children peeped out from under the canvas tops.

These strange people made camp near Eaglefeathers' village. Some of the villagers stood a short distance away watching them.

Eaglefeathers said:

"They are not Jujkam.

So they must be Miliga·n."

Jujkam means Mexicans in our language and Miliga·n means white people.

Eaglefeathers tried to talk in sign-language to these people but they could not understand. So he and his villagers went back to their homes leaving the white campers to themselves.

Somewhere along the way, these white people had heard of the friendly Pima Indians so they were not afraid. They came over to the Indian camp with cloth and beads, and the Pimas gave them all they could eat. The beads pleased the Pimas, but to help these strangers pleased them more. That is how Pimas are. They have never been good traders. For centuries the rich soil and water from the Gila had always given them all they needed. It was easy for them to be generous.

This was the first meeting of white people with the Pima Indians.

After these first travelers had gone on their way, others came. They came into this part of the country so fast that other tribes did not like it and began to make raids on the white immigrants. The raids got so bad after a while that the government found it necessary to establish military posts out here to protect their white people.

One of these posts was established among the Pimas, at Maricopa Wells. Others were established in the Apache country at McDowell and Fort Apache and other places. These posts played an important part in bringing friendly terms between different tribes of Indians, as well as between whites and Indians. They became the center of activities for all.

At first these Army people did not understand the Pimas. They considered anyone who wore so little clothing and lived in houses made of arrow-weed to be savages. They thought that Indians who were generous and friendly must be that way because they were afraid. Pimas never move very fast even when they are working hard, so the early white people thought they were lazy.

But after a while the Army began to understand that a Pima was not an Apache, that not all Indian tribes were alike. Whites and Pimas began to learn each other's language and soon there was a different feeling between them. The white women discovered that the Pima's natural civilization was not so different from what they were trying to teach their own children.

Every so often the Pima parents lectured to their children regarding manhood and womanhood. The boys were told how they must learn to plant crops and how to be good warriors as well as being useful around the home.

The girls were also taught how to be useful around the home. Early in the morning of each day a young woman was up grinding wheat on the metate as she made flour for the coming day.

She also went to the well or spring, often a mile away, with a three gallon olla on her head, and carried water to be used at the camp. She did a number of tasks before the sun was up. She was also taught how to prepare the morning meal with different foods. She was taught the care of a baby by looking after her married sister's baby if there was no other baby in her house.

The boys went after the stock and carried wood to the camp. From day to day these young people were taught the Pima ways of life and grew up to be useful men and women. They were never spanked or struck.

After a while even the Army began to understand that the Pimas were not savages, and could be useful to them.

EARLY DAYS

GRAYHORSE, Swift Arrow and Keli•hi were now grown to young manhood. Keli•hi had married a young girl by the name of Rainbow's Ends. He took her to his home, where she helped his parents, Eaglefeathers and Juana Losso, in all their activities.

In those days, when any one died in a village where everyone was related, all the villagers set fire to their half dozen houses and moved to a new location.

So it happened that death struck the camp of Eaglefeathers. The whole camp was set afire and the villagers moved west of Pima Butte. Sometimes they moved just a short distance and kept on farming their old fields. If they moved a long distance away they would clear a new piece of ground to grow their crops. But always they stayed along the banks of the Gila River.

They were scattered along the Gila River from a little west of Pima Butte to as far east as what was then known as Blackwater, Chukma-shu•dk.

The spreading out of these Pimas along the Gila River was possible because of the coming of the white soldiers who had settled things down to peaceful living.

The Apache raids had stopped. The Pony Express was put in operation. The Pony Express did not last long after the Stage Coach took up the carrying of the mail as well as passengers.

The Stage Coach ran through the Pima Villages, making rest stops at Maricopa Wells. The stage would stop here long enough for passengers to get food before going on.

Sometimes when Eaglefeathers was not working in his field or out hunting, he and some of the boys would go over to visit at Maricopa Wells.

It was on one of these visits that an incident took place:

One of the Pima warriors on seeing the fire-arms used by the white soldiers, thought that the next time he went over to the Wells, he would take his war weapons along and show them to the white soldiers. So the next time he went, he took along his war-club and shield. The soldiers on seeing his weapons, laughed and made all sorts of remarks as to the effective use of such weapons. The joking went on until the Pima made a challenge to the white man. He said:

"You, white warrior
Take shooting iron.
Stand here ready.
I take war club and shield,
Step off ten paces,
Turn around, come back.
If you see any part of me,
Shoot!"

The white soldier stood there with gun in hand while the Pima walked away ten paces, turned around and came back hiding behind the shield so well that no part of his body could be seen. The white soldier did not shoot as the Pima came up to him. With the edge of his shield the Pima knocked the gun out of the soldier's hand. He lifted his war club as if he was about to use it. But the soldier took to his heels and ran into a nearby house, closing the door after him.

The people who saw this show had a good laugh and no such challenge was ever made again.

Sometimes there would be shooting contests between Pimas and whites, Pimas with their bows and arrows and the whites with their firearms. They would place a target at different distances and see who could hit the bull's eye. The Pimas often won the match. They often won prizes of a pair of Army pants or a coat.

At other times, foot races were held at the Post. The Pimas always won the long distance races, but lost the short dashes.

Then someone would say:

"It's time for the stage!"

They would all look toward the east to see if they could see any dust.

"Yes, there it comes!

See the dust just below Pima Butte?"

The liveryman would hurry to the corral to harness the horses to be used on the next lap.

The cook would put on a clean apron, and spread a clean tablecloth over the wooden boards of the table.

He would look at his cooking, and then join the others watching the dust of the stage.

At last they could see the stage coming in sight! The horses at full gallop, the coach swaying back and forth as the wheels hit a rut in the road. With a hissing noise of brakes the coach came to a stop. The passengers got out and stretched themselves, brushing the dust off their clothes.

The cook would come to the door and holler:

"Come and get it!"

When the passengers heard this, they all went over to eat.

While the passengers were eating, the hot horses were unhitched and a new team put in their place.

After the passengers had eaten their meal, they visited around a while before they got on the stage again and started on their way westward. When the stage had gone, the Pimas would go home and everything was quiet again at the Post.

The Pimas learned to do many things by watching these white people. They also picked up a little of their language by listening to their conversation.

PIMA GAMES

SOMETIMES, in the evenings, the young boys would gather up a company to play soldiers. One of the Pima boys had learned enough of the different commands to play the captain. There would also be a sergeant to call the roll.

The sergeant would call out:

"Grayhorse!" and little Grayhorse would answer "he-i," imitating the soldiers.

"Swift Arrow!" and Swift Arrow would say, "he-r-r-r-i!", and so on down the line until all the boys had their names called out.

Then the captain would say, "ten-shun!" Everybody would slap their hands to their sides, throw out their chests and snap their heads back. Then the captain would march down the line looking very stern. All of a sudden he would yell, "dismiss," and everyone would run here and there laughing and joking.

One of the boys had found an old gun-barrel which he used as a bugle and they say he could play the "Reveille" on it as good as any white man on an army bugle. Some of the army clothes they won in contests were used in playing soldiers. Those with stripes down the sides of the pants were most in demand.

Other times they played some of their own games such as "going to see the coyote" or *ban-madr-che·gio* as the Pimas called it. This game was played by very young Pima Indian children.

A group of children line up in single file with hands holding on to the one in front and marching towards another, usually a boy, lying down pretending to be asleep away from the crowd. When they reach the place where the boy is lying asleep, they march around him singing, *alha, alha.* When they have marched four times around him the leader pokes the sleeping boy in the ribs and he jumps up and tries to catch one of the children in the line. The business of the leader of the lines is to prevent the coyote from catching one of the children. The coyote and the leader struggle while the line of children sways back and forth to keep from being caught.

When the coyote grabs one of the children he runs off with him or her and that means he is supposed to have eaten him or her up. When he comes back, another coyote is lying asleep and the game is played over again. The first one caught by the coyote will be the next in turn to lie asleep as the coyote.

We played this game when I was a boy, but the game is not any longer played among the Pima children. Now they play "London Bridge is Falling Down."

Sometimes a *toka* contest was held between two villages. *Toka* is played only by the women. It is like hockey. Sticks about six feet long were used to throw a pair of small wooden balls tied together about three inches apart with a string of raw-hide. A team is ten or more women on each side.

They pick up the set of balls with the end of the stick and toss it as far as they can. Another on that team will toss it again if she can, and run after her toss, until she gets it over the goal line. The playing field is a hundred steps long and fifty steps wide.

When an argument arises they often use the sticks to settle it.

Once in a while a foot race was run with another village. Usually the races were run with a small wooden ball which they picked up with their foot and kicked ahead as they ran. A distance of ten miles was considered a short race in those days.

In dry weather the feed for the stock might be poor nearby, so the Pima boy would take one of these wooden balls along and drive the stock many miles away where the feed was good. Then, kicking the ball, he would run back home.

When the harvest was good and the food was all stored, the Pimas sometimes held a dance. They would dance to songs sung by a group of singers. Usually one person made up the song and taught it to others who helped him sing for the dance.

THE APACHE WARS

AFTER the establishment of the military posts, everything settled down to friendly terms. There was no more fighting between tribes. Only a few of the Apaches were still war-like.

Eaglefeathers took advantage of the peace among the Indians and ventured away from his old home near Pima Butte, looking for new land to farm. He found some good land farther west, ten miles down the Gila River at Gila Crossing.

He had lived long enough west of Pima Butte to see the coming of the white man, the Pony Express and the Stage Coach.

He had lived there long enough to see the white man's way of living change some of the old ways. Pimas now wore some clothes.

Other Pimas moved away from Pima Butte, taking up new land, going over to the Salt River Valley. Others went to a place east and north of what is now Tempe. This settlement was called S-a'al-kuig, which means "little mesquite trees." There they farmed and hunted and fished in the Salt River. S-a'al-kuig is now known as the Salt River Indian Reservation.

Other Pimas went east up the Gila River beyond what was then known as Chukma-shu·dk, meaning Blackwater. These Pimas now occupy an area of land known as U·s-ke·k, which means "Stick-standing."

The O'obab who lived across the Gila River from Pima Butte moved to the Salt River Valley. They are now called Maricopas. They took up land west and south of Phoenix along the Salt River. Phoenix at that time was a small town with only a few houses, but more and more people were coming out there from the east. The growth of the town caused these O'obab to move farther west until they settled where they now live.

From their new home at Gila Crossing Eagle-feathers and some of the villagers often visited Maricopa Wells to see old friends from around Pima Butte.

On one of these visits to the Wells, the officer in charge called one of the Pima boys into his office and said he had an important message that he would like to be delivered at Fort McDowell, but could not spare any of his men to make the trip. The officer wanted to know could the Pima boy make the trip?

The Pima boy said he could.

So the officer fitted him out with a mule to ride and told him that the men at the Fort might shoot at him when he got there! He gave the boy a white cloth and told him, if the men started shooting at him, to wave the white cloth.

The Pima boy started out on the mule and when he got to Fort McDowell, sure enough the soldiers started shooting at him. He took out the white cloth and waved it. They stopped shooting and he delivered the message and came back the next day.

If the Pima boys were asked to do this kind of a job they would do it. But they were glad when the telegraph lines were put in soon after this. The telegraph line connecting Fort McDowell and points west passed through Maricopa Wells. But that wasn't the end of the Pimas doing jobs for the Army.

The Apaches had settled down to peaceful living with the exception of a few leaders and their followers such as the Apache Kid, Cochise and Geronimo.

The government tried all sorts of ways to capture these bands and get them under control. But these Apaches had strong hideouts and would go into them to get away from the soldiers. So the government found it necessary to employ other Indians to track them down.

Some of the Pimas, Maricopas and Apaches were mustered into the U. S. Army for that purpose. With their knowledge of the country these Indian troops soon brought Geronimo and the others under control. Cochise never was caught. When he was surrounded by the troops, he rode his horse over a cliff and died that way.

Sometimes you hear people say: "Those Apaches were bad." I don't know. They are peaceful people today, doing a good job with their livestock.

In the early days they did cause the Pimas, and others, some trouble. We had plenty from our farms and those Apaches only had what they could hunt over their wild mountains. Sometimes they would come down

47

and raid us and we fought them back away from our settlements and then left them alone. They never tried to drive us off our land and away from our homes. We never tried to drive them out of their own country.

But the white man did.

If you were an Apache what do you think you would have done?

Which reminds me of a certain incident:

One time up in Prescott, a group of Indians went into a restaurant to eat. They sat down at a table and ordered a big meal. They were very hungry. When the waiter brought the food, they ate heartily.

At the next table to them sat some white people. After watching these Indians eat, one of them said:

"I wish I had that Indian's appetite!"

One Indian heard him and said:

"What's matter?

You take land! You take water!

Now, you want my appetite! What for?"

All through the time the whites moved westward, there were Indian wars. Because somebody wanted something somebody else had. This was true among Indian tribes that fought each other. It was true when the whites moved west. It must be true among nations.

PROGRESS

THE government agency established at Sacaton served all the Indians along the Gila River as well as along the Salt River. A little later, these Indian villages were set aside as a Reservation.

Up to that time most of the Pimas and Maricopas wore long hair. One of the first steps towards their "civilization" was to get them to cut their hair. Finding this a difficult problem, the agency offered a hat to anyone who cut his hair.

Also at that time the Pimas and Maricopas were still using the *olas-ki* (round house) although a few built square houses from cactus ribs, plastered over with mud.

The agency tried to get them to build adobe houses. But they soon found out that all these improvements could not be made unless the Indian was educated. A number of Pimas were sent east to school. Some went to Santa Fe, Albuquerque, Grand Junction and Carlisle. Some stayed a few months, some a few years before they managed to get back home. It is said that some Pimas who went to an eastern school for two months came home thinking they had forgotten their own language.

They would stammer: "Wha-wa-wa-sha" for *huas-ha'a* which means "plate" in Pima. But they remembered the words for what went on a plate. Pretty soon they were speaking the language as good as any other Pima.

The agency had a hard time getting those Pimas to give up their *olas-ki* to build and live in adobe houses. Adobe houses were supposed to be more civilized than the old arrow-weed shelters. But the Pimas did not want to change. So the agency issued a wagon to any Pima family who would build and live in an adobe house. The only thing was, they forgot to issue plans, so a Pima who wanted a free wagon built an adobe house according to his old ideas of a house, with a small door and no windows. These were warm on the few cold nights, but there was no ventilation.

Some older people in my own family did what the agency told them to do. They built and lived in an adobe house. When they died they all died of tuberculosis.

Our people now build good houses with plenty of windows. All those early ones were abandoned many years ago. You can still see the ruined walls of some of them on the Reservation.

Near the foothills of the Estrella Mountains, Eaglefeathers made his final home. He was now along in years and no more able to carry on the affairs of his village. Keli•hi was selected to take his place.

Across the Santa Cruz River from where Eaglefeathers lived were the farms of Grayhorse, Swift Arrow and Keli•hi. This settlement is still called Hya-thob meaning that the people who live there are Pimas who came from east of Pima Butte.

Keli•hi often went to Sacaton to consult Chief

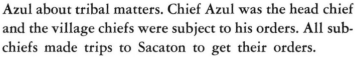

Azul about tribal matters. Chief Azul was the head chief and the village chiefs were subject to his orders. All sub-chiefs made trips to Sacaton to get their orders.

The ruins of Chief Azul's house can still be seen to the right as you enter the town of Sacaton from the north — a two story structure with the roof fallen in. In front, across the road to the south is a monument which was put up in memory of the first Indian killed in World War One who was a Pima Indian from our tribe.

As time went on, a missionary came to preach to the Pimas. Charles H. Cook was the first missionary and made his headquarters at Sacaton. The Pimas were slow to grasp the white man's religion. But once they understood it they became faithful believers.

Pimas who were converted at Gila Crossing would journey forty-five miles to Sacaton every weekend to attend church. It took almost two days each way to make the trip on foot.

Today the name Dr. Cook is still respected throughout the Pima villages. At Sacaton there is a large church built in his memorial.

When the Railroad had just been built along the south side of the Gila River, connecting California to the east, it was a great sight to the Pimas to see the engine coming along the tracks. Some of them would run around the corner of a house for fear the engine would swallow them.

After a while they got used to it, and the traincrew men would ask the Pimas to get on and go for a ride, and they would get on and go down to Yuma or up to Tucson. They did this for a while but the trains got into a wreck so often, killing some of the Pimas riding on them, that the government put a stop to it.

Grayhorse, Swift Arrow and Keli•hi were now busy on their new farms at Gila Crossing, or Santa Cruz Village as it is now called.

The people of this village had dug a canal from the river to their farms. When a brush-dam would wash out they would build another.

In those days there was always a good stream flowing in the Gila River. They were never out of irrigating water and the crops were always good.

About this time there was born of Keli•hi and Rainbow's Ends a son. They named him Buzzing Feather.

At the time Buzzing Feather was born, Keli•hi and Rainbow's Ends had five other children.

Here I might as well tell you who the characters are whose names appear in this writing:

Eaglefeathers was my grandfather, Juana Losso my grandmother.

Grayhorse and Swift Arrow were my uncles.

Keli•hi was my father, and Rainbow's Ends was my mother.

So Buzzing Feather, just now come into the story, is myself!

52

THOSE WHO ARE GONE

HUHUGAM is a Pima word meaning "Those Who are Gone." It is sometimes written Ho-ho-kam, and is the Pima name for those people who came into our desert country thousands of years ago. No one knows where they came from, or what became of them. I think, as all Papagos and Pimas do, that we are their descendants.

I remember an old Pima we buried a few years ago. His name was Tash-kuint, which means "Counting the Suns." All during his life he never cut his hair. He always wore it long. He was the only Pima I ever saw who kept his hair long. He never slept one night except outdoors or in some arrow-weed *olas-ki* he built here and there along the Gila Valley. The only foods he would eat were the old Indian foods prepared from the sahuaro cactus fruits or sprouts of the cholla cactus or mesquite beans, or small game that he caught or killed.

Old Tash-kuint could remember the signs that were carved on the Calendar Stick and tell about old events so that you would think you were there. One time he told me that he was well acquainted with Ho'ok,

Eagleman, White Clay Eater and all the other spirits in Pima legend.

Tash-kuint was a wise old man, in many ways. But when he was a hundred and fifteen years old he died like anybody else.

When I remember Tash-kuint I think I know what those old Huhugam were like.

Also I think of my grandfather, Eaglefeathers, as one of them. And my father, Keli•hi, whose name meant "Old Fashioned." To those Pimas of my childhood the past was not so far away.

What I have already told in this writing was told to me by those "People Who are Gone." It was the old ones who told me the legends I will write down before I am finished. Some of these things you will not find in any book but are known only by us, the Pima Indians.

There is one day I remember. It was raining. Grayhorse, and Swift Arrow and Keli•hi went over to the *olas-ki* of their father, Eaglefeathers, my grandfather. They told me about their visit late that night when they came home again.

As they went into the *olas-ki,* old Eaglefeathers was lying on his bed singing in a low voice. On seeing his boys come in, he stopped singing and struggled to sit up. With the help of his boys he sat up and reached for a drink of water. After drinking he said:

"I was hoping that you would come over as I have something to say to you."

Then he said:

Many moons, many suns
Have come and gone.
With patience and hardship
I have gone through life

To bring you up to what you are today.
The coming of the white man
Has made much change in your lives,
And will make more changes.
So, go! Go ahead with what has come.
Send your children to school
To learn the white man's ways
That they may have proper dealings with him.
Because if you don't
He will get the best of the deal.
My time will not be much longer.
Go through the remainder of your days
Treating everyone fair
That you may be treated the same.
When you come to the road to the
Singing and dancing grounds,
You will have nothing to regret, knowing
That you have done your part while here.

After saying this, Eaglefeathers laid himself back
on his bed and began to sing. When I was older my
father taught me that song.

This is what Eaglefeathers sang:

The earth was just made.
Upon it grew beautiful flowers.
As I saw the earth, my heart brightened.
I began to sing a song of praise
To the One who made this earth.

Buzzing Feather was about four years old when Eaglefeathers died. Juana Losso soon followed. They were very old. They were buried on the banks of the Santa Cruz River near Santa Cruz Village.

Not long ago I went there. As I sat on the grave my thoughts went back to my childhood days. Then all at once the idea came to me, to do what I have done. To write the stories you have read, which were events that took place during the lifetime of those old people.

Now, I will try to relate events that took place during my own time.

BOYHOOD

BUZZING Feather's boyhood was spent at the Santa Cruz Village where his father, Keli·hi, had his farm. Like any other Pima boy, Buzzing Feather had certain assigned duties to do on the farm. One of those duties was to see that the stock was watered. When there was no water in the ditch they had to be driven to the Santa Cruz River a quarter of a mile away.

Watering the stock was one chore I liked because when the stock was very thirsty, as soon as I let them out of the gate, they would jump and kick their heels up in the air, then run all the way to the water. I would follow at full speed on my pony!

Carrying wood into the house was a chore I did not like as well, because sometimes I got mesquite thorns in my bare feet.

After these chores were done, some of the boys would come to the house and we would go fishing or hunting. Sometimes we would climb mountains.

We lived in one of those adobe houses. Like all Pima homes it faced east. A Pima house always faced east because the door was the only opening for the sun to shine in when it came up in the morning.

In front of the house was a *vato* and in the rear another arrow-weed house. About fifty yards away toward the west were the corrals, sheds and the store-house.

57

Next to the corrals were stacks of hay for the stock. In the sheds were the wagons and other implements.

To the north side of the house was a small orchard of about a dozen trees, mostly apricots. I remember the first time these apricots ripened. Keli•hi had given us strict orders not to go into the orchard to eat apricots until they were good and ripe. But we, like any other children, would go into the orchard when he was away and eat green apricots. By the time he got back, we would be all doubled up with a tummy-ache.

He would laugh at us and say:

"You will know better next time!"

And we did know better, too. We would never go into the orchard unless we were told to, to pick fruit for my mother, Rainbow's Ends.

Rainbow's Ends would dry the apricots on racks in the sun. No one told us not to pass by the racks, so we would pass by them very often until our stomachs told us that we had better think of something else to do.

Keli•hi farmed about forty acres. He also owned some horses and cattle. Some of the horses ran on the range with the cattle. When the cows had calves we would bring one or two in to milk.

We also had a corral on the range where we camped. We would gather what cows had calves, feed them a little hay and put their calves in a small corral so the cows would come in from the range to feed them. We would then milk the cows, feeding the calves part of the milk. We would camp at the corral for several days milking and making cheese.

The Pony Express, the Stage Coach and the telegraph lines that passed through Maricopa Wells were all things of the past. The wires that held together the gate posts on our corral were some pieces of the old telegraph wires.

When we grew older and ventured farther away from home we would go to Maricopa Wells to see the trains as they went by. We would stay there for hours watching the engine switching cars from one track to another. We had to hurry home to do our work on the farm, sometimes after dark.

After the harvest was over, the grain put away, there would always be some grain left over which must be taken to the mill or market. My folks would load it on a wagon and make a trip to Phoenix. Sometimes they would take me along.

I remember the first time I went to Phoenix. At that time there was a grocery store at the southwest corner of Washington and First Streets, where we used to get our groceries. I think it was called J. W. Dorris.

Buzzing Feather would stand there, his mouth wide open, watching little cups go back and forth on wires stretched overhead and connected to a booth in the rear part of the store.

When you gave some money to the man waiting on you, he would reach up, take down a little cup from the wires, put the money in it and place it back on the wires. Then he would get hold of a string that hung down from the wires, give it a yank, and away the little cup would go up to the booth. After a while the little cup would come running back. With a clicking noise it would come to a stop. The clerk would reach up again, take down the little cup and give the customer his change.

Buzzing Feather stood there for hours watching this and smelling the grocery store smell of coffee being ground until Rainbow's Ends finished buying what she needed and dragged him away.

In those days, it took us three days to make the trip of eighteen miles to Phoenix and back. On the first day, we would get as far as the canal which ran along the south side of the Salt River. There we would camp for the night under the cottonwoods. The next day we would go on into town and do our shopping. That evening we would go back and camp again at the same place. The third day we would start for home as the sun came up. Our home was on the other side of the mountains.

The sun goes down behind those mountains early, especially in the winter. One of the Pimas living on the upper part of the river once made this remark:

"It is noon here, but right now the people at Santa Cruz Village are shaking out their blankets getting ready to go to bed!"

This will give you an idea how close we lived to the Estrella Mountains.

SCHOOL DAYS

ACROSS the Gila River from where we lived the government built a school house. Buzzing Feather and the children from Santa Cruz Village were among the first to go to school there. My memories go back to those days. Each morning Rainbow's Ends would fix us a pail of lunch and we would walk three miles to the school house. We had to cross the Gila River on our way.

There was always a stream of water running about two feet deep and twenty feet wide. The river bed itself was three-fourths of a mile wide with a heavy growth of cottonwood, willow and arrow-weeds. We would follow a trail through this brush without any thought of wild animals. Nothing ever bothered us except one time there were some cattle in the river. The bull was known to be very mean. We all picked up good sized sticks. When the bull saw us, he made a deep bass noise and came toward us. We were taught never to run from a bull. So Buzzing Feather stood there with his stick raised. The bull came on and when it got close enough, Buzzing Feather jumped to one side, at the same time hitting the bull on the nose. While we all ran on toward the school we could hear that bull a mile away still blowing his nose. Buzzing Feather felt very proud of himself. But that was one day he arrived early at school.

We used to take off our shoes to wade across

the water in the river. In the summer time we liked to do this. But in the winter we used to hate it, the water was so cold. One time we took some lard from my mother's kitchen and greased our shoes and the legs of our pants with it to keep the water out. We discovered that our legs and feet got just as wet and the lard made a mess in the warm schoolhouse when it melted, but our feet stayed cold and wet all day. We found out that it was not a very good idea, but we were always trying something.

In the spring the water was fine and after school we would pull off our clothes and swim a while before going on home.

One time Buzzing Feather had another idea. He brought an old axe from the wood pile at home and left it down by the river. The next day, instead of going on to school, he and another boy stayed at the river playing all day. At noon we ate our school lunch, and in the afternoon when the other children came by on their way home we put on a show for them. I climbed to the top of a willow that stood near the edge of the water and out on a leaning branch while the other boy chopped the branch off and I fell into the water with the branch.

It was such fun that everybody had to take turns being chopped down. We did this all day long for several days, stopping our game only to chase a fish when we saw one. Once one of the boys slipped on a wet stone and fell on a fish and stunned it, so we cooked it and ate it.

Then, one day, the teacher came to our house!

He asked Keli•hi what the reason was for me not attending school.

Father said:

"He goes every day!"

The teacher shook his head and said:

"Buzzing Feather has not been to school for the last three days."

I was peeping from around the corner of the house. Keli•hi saw me and said:

"Son! Come here!"

When I came, he asked me if what the teacher said about missing school was true.

Buzzing Feather said it was.

Keli•hi turned to the teacher and said:

"Teacher!

My boy will be there tomorrow!"

The next day Buzzing Feather rode behind Keli•hi on a horse's back to school. This made him feel ashamed. But Keli•hi seemed to enjoy the ride. He sang all the way.

THE GREAT WHEAT HARVEST

THE Pima and Papago Indians have always been known for their hospitality.

If you came to the home of another Pima, no matter what time of day, the first thing placed before you would be some kind of food. When you had travelled a long distance, your team was taken care of with water and feed.

When Pimas visit among each other, when the visiting party leaves, they are given beans, corn, cactus syrup or melons to take home. If you have a patch of melons, you will have visitors from all parts of the Reservation.

The Pimas did not sell much of their farm produce, but stored it away for food and seed.

In the store room there would be three or four large size storage baskets. There would be smaller baskets and ollas full of mesquite bean cakes, balls of cactus fruit, cactus seeds, dried meat in sacks, cheese and salt. In one corner, stacked in straw, would be musk melons, watermelons, and pumpkins. Hanging from the ceiling would be bundles of fox-tail weed, split willow branches and devil claws for basket making.

In those days the Pimas always had plenty.

The Papagos who lived in the desert south of us did not have a river like the Gila to water their fields, and their food was never plentiful.

During the summer months, some of them would come to our village, with cactus syrup put up in little ollas, and salt, and we would give them beans and corn in exchange.

The only salt we had came from the Papagos. At a certain time of the year they would go down to the ocean and get the salt from the shore where the tide left the water to dry. It was a kind of ceremony with them.

They always felt that we gave them more than they could give us, although to get the salt they had walked hundreds of miles to the ocean and back. And so they would stay with us for a few days and help us harvest our wheat.

These Papagos cut wheat with a sickle, putting the cut grain into little piles as they go along. After they have finished a field of grain, a wagon goes along with everybody using pieces of small sized rope about three feet long to tie the wheat into bundles, throwing them on the wagon.

The man on the wagon unties a bundle, placing the cut grain so he can get as much on the wagon as he can. It is interesting to watch these Papagos joking and laughing as they work.

After the wagon is loaded, it is taken to a threshing place and the load dumped off. This threshing place is usually made in the field, close by, so the wagon does not have to go too far to unload.

In making one of these threshing places, the ground is cleared, leveled, sprinkled, and a long pole is put up in the center. The wheat, cut about two feet long, is dumped around this pole.

After the cut wheat is stacked, three or four horses are tied loosely to the center pole and are driven around the stake, round and round until the grain is tramped out. When the grain is tramped out, the straw is thrown up into the air to separate the chaff from the grain. This is done with a little wind blowing.

The women, putting a cloth over their heads and back, use arrow-weeds to sweep off anything that falls with the grain. These women are doing this while the grain and straw is being thrown into the air. You can see the usefulness of the cloth over their heads and back.

Sometimes a wind blows at night so, if there is a bright moon, the people do all this at night. They usually do this for part of the night, but if there is a good wind and bright moonlight some people thresh all night.

Early in the morning they would break up their camp in the field. Bundles and bags were scattered all over the camp grounds. The Papagos had nets that went over the horse's back and hung down on either side in which they put their goods. Then they piled their bedding on and sat on top of that.

After everything was packed on the animals, the Papagos would go around shaking hands with us, then help each other mount, and say:

"We go now! If everything is all right with us we'll be back next year."

Then they would string out along the road and start their homeward journey. We would stand there watching those good people until they disappeared from sight. When only the dust could be seen we would all go back to the house.

Some years later I happened to accompany a missionary making a trip throughout the Papago country. We stopped at a certain village to ask an elderly lady about the road.

After directing us, she asked me where I was from. I told her. Making a little pleased noise she asked who my parents were. I told her. She jumped up, grabbed my shoulders, looking me square in the eyes and said:

"Buzzing Feather!

You were a small boy when we used to come to your place to cut wheat. That was many years ago. I am your aunt. This is the village where your grandparents on your mother's side lived. Over there, lives another aunt." And she pointed out several places where my relations lived.

Many Pima and Papago families are related because of those many times the Papagos came to help us harvest our wheat.

This is a song the Papago Indians like to sing when they go traveling around somewhere:

They have gone,
The birds of the sky.
They have gone,
The animals of the earth,
They have returned
Along their own trail.

On a white rock under the moon,
On a red rock under the sun,
On a black rock they sat,
On a yellow rock they rested
And looked back and saw butterflies,
They looked behind them and saw
A whirlwind,
And they watched the whirlwind
And it was a tree
Standing in a cool shadow.

They sit under the tree in the shadow,
They sit under the still tree.

FLOOD

WHEN there were heavy rains on the upper part of the Gila, it would cause the river to raise with high water. Then, we would have an excuse to miss school. No one could cross the river. The muddy water would run for days, sometimes a week. It would sweep whole trees along with it and boulders would grind over each other. These were times when hundreds of frogs would come out of the mud and you would hear them all night long. You would think they were sheep bleating.

When this high water ran for any length of time, some of the Pimas at Santa Cruz would run out of groceries. There were no grocery stores in the villages at that time and all our supplies were bought in Phoenix. So the people would set a day and all gather at the river bank.

Some of the men would take their clothes off, then, with a hand full of long arrow-weeds they would wade into the water, placing the sticks along a course they thought would be a good place for a crossing, safe from quicksand.

After the sticks had been placed, the boys would get on their horses and ride back and forth over this marked course to pack the loose sand so the wagons would not go down in quicksand when they crossed.

When the sand was packed down, the team that

was to make the trip to town was unhitched and driven across. Then the wagon, sometimes loaded with grain, was taken hold of by twenty-five or thirty men and they would pull it across the river. Sometimes the water would be waist deep and swift.

After the wagons were pulled across, the teams would be hitched on again and they would go on their way to town. Sometimes there would be a half-dozen wagons pulled across in this manner.

After they were on their way we would all go home. In two days we would go back to the crossing and wait for the wagons to return. When they came, they were pulled across the same way. Sometimes the water would be so swift that the boys on the upper side of the wagon would be knocked over and the water would carry them under the wagon to the other side before they could regain their footing. They would laugh and joke about it, but in the winter time it would be cold.

The older men who did not get in the water would have a bonfire on the bank of the river so the boys could warm themselves and dry their clothes. The ones who made the trip into town would always bring back a pie or cake for those who helped get the wagons across.

THE PIMA LANGUAGE

THE Pimas and the Papagos speak the same language only in a different dialect.

The Papagos call the Pimas *A kimel o'otam* which means "River People." The Pimas call the Papagos *Tohono o'otam* which means "Desert People."

These two tribes have lived close to each other on friendly terms for so long and are so mixed that it is hard to tell which is which, except for the small difference of their dialect.

In these two tribes there are two clans. You can tell who belongs to one clan or the other by the way people speak to their parents. Those who refer to their father as *va·v* or *ma·m* belong to the Buzzard Clan. Those who call their father *'apap* or *apki* you will know belong to the Coyote Clan.

The Buzzards and the Coyotes are not so close together as the Pima Buzzards and the Papago Buzzards, or the Pima Coyotes and the Papago Coyotes. Between the two tribes there are never any hard words. But sometimes people who belong to the opposite clan get into an argument. If you could hear one of these arguments you would get some good laughs. Especially between two married people belonging to the opposite clans.

We have no bad swear words in our language. Words like *ashu·ge-nuwi,* (you stinking little Buzzard), or *alu·ge-ban,* (you sneaky old Coyote), are about the worst I can think of.

Also, we have no greeting words. When we meet someone we just ask him: *paptohi,* (where you going?) When going visiting and not finding anyone at home we say loudly: *nam'ia va·dadrha,* (are you there?) You will find these phrases very effective. The next time you meet a Pima, just say: *paptohi.* If he is not at home, be sure to say: *nam'ia va·dadrha.*

In any language, it is a wonderful thing to hear a child call you "grandpa."

Some of my grandchildren call me *vosk* and some of them call me *ba·ba'a.* That is because in Pima the children of sons call their grandfather *vosk,* and the children of daughters call him *ba·ba'a.* A child who speaks only English must be very confused when he meets his two grandfathers and has to call them both by the same name.

In Pima, a grandmother is called *ga·ga'a* or *lu·lu'u* to make the same distinction.

The Pimas are very exact about relationships.

I am told that our language is similar to the Hopi language and also to the language spoken by the old Aztecs of Mexico. If this means that the Pima Indians are related to these tribes, I think we are more pleased to be related to the peaceful Hopis than to the Aztecs.

Not all of anyone's relatives turn out the same. I like some of my own Pima relatives more than I like some others. I am most partial to the ones who call me *vosk* or *ba·ba'a.*

Those are my twenty-four grandchildren.

In our tribe today many young Pimas speak English altogether. But they still speak Pima to their small children. It is a very gentle and musical language.

One time I happened to be talking with a member of our tribe who was married to a white man. Knowing that they speak English at all times I asked:

"After speaking English all these years, can you still talk Pima?"

She looked at me in surprise and said: *a shat 'e ju·kuniso pi-neokad,* (Why shouldn't I?)

Anyone, once speaking the language, will not ever forget it.

In some homes both Pima and English are spoken so mixed together you can hardly tell what they are talking about.

One time I was at a friend's house where I was invited to eat dinner. The lady of the house took her place at one end of the table with her husband at the other end and placed me in the middle. After grace, the lady said to me:

"George! Help yourself and please pass me the *churrmith* and butter."

It would have been easier to say bread and butter. Anyway, the word in pure Pima is *che-mait,* not *churrmith.*

The Pimas of old times used some words that the Pimas of today do not use. For instance, I was at a certain gathering where someone used an old expression, *shahali'i*. Some of the boys near me heard the word and asked me what it meant.

I told them it was an old Pima word meaning "all right then," the same as when you say, "All right then, I'll do it." In Pima one would ·say: *Mant 'abo va n-ju·, shahali'i,* (I will do it then.)

The young Pimas just say: "Okay."

When meeting, sometimes they ask: *shapa'i chu'ig?* (How are you?), or if they are real modern, *shap kaij?* (What do you say?)

This greeting has come into use because they have heard white people use it when they meet. When you meet a Pima, it is better to say *shapa'i chu'ig,* than just "How!"

We have no written books of our language, but a little association with Pima-speaking people will, in a short time, enable one to speak the Pima language.

Many white people in the towns surrounding the Reservation speak Pima very well. The Chinese merchants in these towns speak our language better than the white people.

I recall a time, not long ago, we were in a Chinese store in a certain town near the Reservation. We were looking for some kind of dessert. The Chinese clerk came up and asked us what we were looking for. We told him. He picked up a strawberry preserve and to our surprise he said in plain Pima: *Go 'ep sitoli we·nags 'i·da,* (This is pretty good. It has syrup in it.) We asked him where he learned to speak Pima so well?

He said: "Right here in this town. I grew up here and learned to speak the language by playing and talking with Pimas and Papagos ever since I was a boy."

I know of other Chinese who speak our language almost better than some Pimas do these days.

HORSE ROUND-UP

THIRTY miles south of Phoenix, about three miles north from the east end of the Estrella Mountains, there lies a mesquite thicket so heavy with a growth of trees that it is impossible for a man to ride a horse through except in certain places. Here and there it is cut up with washes and gullies, some with running water in them, others with a boggy bottom, making it difficult to cross on horseback. But the animals that run in this thicket know many lanes that wind across it in every direction.

When the Pima Indians heard about the City of New York having so many buildings that it must look like a jungle, they called this place crowded with trees and animals New York Thicket.

With desert and mountains all around, New York Thicket is about three miles wide north to south and eight miles long east and west. When cattle were plentiful, as well as horses, three to four thousand head of stock ran in and around this thicket. That was between 1900 and 1915. Today, I don't think there are a hundred head of cattle and horses running there, but it is a great refuge for coyotes, badger, bob cats, porcupine, javelina, mountain lion, and deer. And rattlesnakes. Whitewing doves breed and nest there during the summer months.

In the early days, the south end of this thicket,

about a mile wide and two miles long was swampy and covered with a heavy growth of bamboo which the Pima Indians call *va·pku*. Today there is not so much water, and no bamboo. Water used to come up out of the ground in many places and I am told that this is where Arizona got its name. The Indians called this place *a'al-sho·shon,* meaning "many springs." There are still places where cattle sometimes bog down. On the edge of this open swampy place the Pimas built their corrals to hold cattle and horses when they held a round-up.

Every year during the spring a round-up was held there to gather and brand horses or cattle. In the villages a man would stand on top of a house and in a loud voice call the people to a meeting to talk about a horse round-up. At the meeting a date is set.

The day before the round-up, the boys move their equipment over to make camp at the corrals. They haul in hay, grain, bedding and cooking utensils with enough food to last two or three days. They dig a well and repair the corrals.

That evening at camp the head round-up boss, Kusho'e-vij, meaning "Wrinkled in the Back of the Head," tells the plans for the coming day. He tells where the horses are to be run, and held up, who is to haul water, and who is to give signals. Then men are selected to captain the riders at different points along the route of the drive. A box canyon at the foot of the Estrella

Mountains is chosen to hold up or catch the horses.

The next morning after breakfast the boys saddled up their horses and rode over to the corrals. The signal man and the waterman were already on their way. At the corrals, Kusho'e-vij told each captain to pick his men and all to take their positions. Then he and his helpers went to a high place where they could watch the drive.

Everybody is waiting for the smoke signal to start the drive.

When the smoke goes up and the riders see it they start riding, yelling, and calling to each other. Soon a little dust rises here and there, increasing until the whole thicket is covered with dust. The boys ride without seeing each other in the dusty thicket, only hearing their yelling above the thunder of hoofs of the running horses. Every now and then an urgent call comes through the trees, *"Kui·va! Kui·va!"* meaning, "West! West!" The horses were headed in the wrong direction!

Now the riders turn the herd toward the west and follow them out of the thicket.

One of the boy's horses falls as it steps in a hole and throws him. The rider jumps up and gets on his mount again and rides on after the running horses.

Soon the boys have all the herd out of the trees and turned and heading out toward the box canyon. A few of us take a rest, while a fresh team takes out after the herd. We get off and loosen the cinches of our saddles. Some take their saddles off so the horses can cool off. They walk their horses back and forth so they will not cool off too quick. Soon we saddle up again and ride over toward the box canyon where the rest of the boys have driven the herd.

When the signal man sees the dust die down he comes down from the hill where he made the signal and also heads over to the box canyon.

As we neared the narrow opening into this canyon, we heard yelling and the pounding of a horse running toward us. A big black stallion had broken out and was running away as fast as it could. The boys were racing to try to turn it back, but the stallion came on. I said to the boys with me:

"I am going to stop that stallion or break my neck trying to!

Get over on the other side of the trail and let him pass between us."

They did and I pulled up behind a little tree that stood beside the trail, making a loop in my rope, intending to catch the stallion's forefeet when he went by and jerk him down. Because I had my eyes on the stallion I did not see an old man on a little buckskin pony riding in to head him off. As the stallion came racing down the trail he stumbled and was struggling to keep on his feet when the old man rode up, right in his path, waving his hands and shouting.

What did I do?

I froze!

If that stallion hit the old man, it would be just too bad. Ten feet away he regained his footing. Just tipping the old man's pony on the rump, the big animal rushed past like a wind and the scared little buckskin sat down on the ground with the old man still in the saddle. The old man didn't say a word. In fact nobody said anything.

The stallion got clean away.

We rode on into the box canyon where the boys were holding about forty head caught in the drive and as we rode in one of the boys said:

"Pretty good catch."

Then Kusho'e-vij said:

"We will have to cross-tie the legs of some of the stallions. They saw the big black get away and some of them are thinking about trying it.

George, you and Charlie get in there and rope while Harry and Jim do the tying."

George and Charlie tighten the cinches to their saddles, get hold of the saddle-horn and pull it back and forth to see if it is firm. As they move into the bunch of horses, Charlie says:

"I'll take the head and you take the hind. Which stallion shall we tackle first?"

George says:

"That big gray over in the corner. He is thinking up some devilment."

So Charlie made a small half-loop and worked his way toward the big gray stallion. When he got close enough he whirled his rope a few times and threw it clean over the head of the big gray who snorted and tried to dodge the loop, but too late. The loop was already tightening around his neck and Charlie was making a few dollies around the saddle-horn. The rest of the herd went milling around. When the way was clear, George hollered to Charlie:

"Now!"

Charlie gave the gray a slake and the big horse thought he was free. He started out to run, to follow the other horses. But George dropped his loop for the stallion to step into and with a quick jerk pulled him down, and Harry and Jim ran up with short ropes and tied his legs. One forefoot was tied to one hind foot short enough so he couldn't run free but he could still walk. They meant to leave him there to pick up later.

After this was done, Kusho'e-vij said:

"Now that we have our horses, move around them close enough so no horse can pass you. But if they do, don't leave your place in the line."

Then the boys drove the horses out of the box canyon toward the corral, one man riding ahead to lead the way to the best crossing of a wash or the best way out of a grove of trees. On they went through the dust until someone yelled:

"Look out!

You in front!"

The boys in front swung out when they saw the big gray stallion coming down the trail. He had broken the ropes tied to his legs and was trying to rush his way through our lines. As he came up on us, he made a rush for the old man on a little buckskin pony, the same old man who had almost been run down before by the black.

The old man was riding with his rope loose around the saddle-horn holding a loop in his hand with which he hit his horse now and then. When the stallion came racing by, he sort of jumped and hit out with his loop and it fell right over the head of the stallion. The loose rope around the old man's saddle-horn became a hard knot. Once more the little buckskin pony sat down on his haunches, but somehow he held the big stallion while everybody yelled:

"Hold him! Hold him!"

Only the old man didn't want to hold him. He was doing all he could to undo the knot on his saddle-horn to let the stallion go.

George and Charlie rode up to help the old man. They roped the stallion and threw him.

Everybody yelled and laughed when the old man said:

"All I tried to do was hit him on the head. I never meant to rope him."

We tied the legs of the gray stallion and started

to move on again. We laughed and talked about the old man and his little buckskin pony all the way back to the corral. We arrived at the corral just as the sun was setting over the top of the Estrella Mountains. When we closed the gate on our rounded-up stock, our day's work was done.

And Kusho'e-vij said:

"You boys did a good job.

Go to your camps and get something to eat."

The boys went to their camps. They unsaddled their mounts, watered and fed them and then built fires and cooked their supper. When we rolled in for sleep we were still talking about the old man and his buckskin pony who roped the biggest stallion in the bunch.

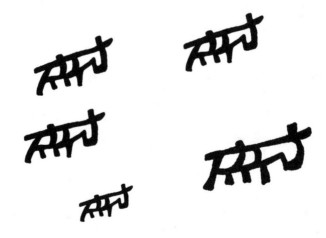

THE MISSION

THE Gospel Mission, established at Sacaton many years ago, soon extended to other villages along the Gila River. A church was built at Gila Crossing about forty-five miles west of Sacaton down the river. My folks were some of the many Pimas who went to this new church. It was there that they received their baptism and were given English names. The name Webb was given to my family. The given name they gave me was George so I am now George Webb.

The Pimas at this time were faithful Christians. All week they would work on their farms and at the end of the week they would go down to the river to wash their clothes and bathe. They would do odd jobs such as cutting wood, so that nothing unnecessary was left to be done on Sunday. On Sunday they would hitch up the team to the spring wagon and pile in it and go to church.

The first person we would see was an elderly gentleman the Pimas called Ba'ihia. He always wore a tall black hat, a white stiff-breasted shirt, a stiff collar with a bow-tie, a black long-tailed coat, knee pants and black stockings. A cane hung over his arm, and he wore white gloves. He stood in front of the pulpit waving his hand, directing people to their seats. I tell you we were seeing somebody when we looked at Ba'ihia!

I remember when some of our boys came home from school back east. How nicely they were dressed in dark blue uniforms with yellow stripes on the arms and down the side of their pants! When they came into the church I pulled on Mother's skirts and asked:

"Who are they?"

She told me that they were some of our boys come home from an eastern school, Carlisle. I joined the others standing around admiring these boy's uniforms and made up my mind that I would like to go to school, too.

My mother would always take something along for me to eat in church. A stick candy or crackers or an apple. In those days we ate in church. It kept the children from going to sleep.

I remember one day the preacher stood up and asked the congregation:

"How many of you would like to go to heaven? All who would like to go to heaven hold up your right hand!"

Everyone in the room held up their hands with the exception of a little boy who sat in the front row.

The preacher noticed that the little boy did not hold up his hand so he asked:

"Little boy! Don't you want to go to heaven?"

The little boy said: "No!"

"Why don't you want to go to heaven?" asked the preacher.

And the little boy said: "Because Mama told me to come right back home after the service."

After the first service, which was what we now call Sunday School, we would all go out for half an hour and visit around with friends. In the summer time we would always have melons along and would invite some of our friends over to the wagon to eat the melons with us. Then the bell would ring and we would all go back into the church.

Before the coming of the Christian religion among the Pimas, their worship had been to a Supreme Being who made the sun and moon.

Religion was natural to us, and so was the moral thinking. Pimas have always thought about matters of proper behavior. When they gave their word of honor it was very important for them to keep it if they could.

One incident shows how they felt about keeping their word:

A Pima bought a new wagon in Phoenix and made a half down payment. The store manager asked him when he would pay the balance. He thought for a while and then he said:

"When the moon is up there," pointing to a certain place in the sky, "I will bring the money."

Later, when the moon was in that part of the sky, this Pima walked into the store.

The manager said:

"Howdy Chief! What makes you so wet?"

The Pima said:

"The Salt River was high and when I came over the crossing in that wagon there was some quicksand, but I told you I would come with the money when the moon was up there, so I did. Here is the money."

As the manager accepted the money, he patted the Pima on the back and said: "Chief! When you need anything else, just ask me!"

So the Pima said:

"I need something right now."

"What?" asked the manager.

"A new wagon," said the Pima. "My other one sank in the quicksand."

Our minister, Mr. Charles H. Cook, was a fine man. But sometimes he was an unwelcomed caller at some homes. As he made his rounds of calling on people and as he approached a certain home, he saw someone move past the window, so he knew someone was home. He rapped on the door but nobody answered. He rapped again and heard someone running to open the door. A little girl peeped out and said:

"Mama told me to tell you that she is not in."

Mr. Cook often laughed about this and told about it from the pulpit, and we all laughed, too. But it wasn't long before that Mama and her family were coming to the church with the rest of us.

Pimas always have a conscience working in them somewhere.

I remember a friend of mine named Grayeagle telling me how he went into a town one night and had some drinks. On his way home through the moonlight he passed by a neighbor's place where there was a big pile of beans ready to thresh.

Grayeagle looked at the beans in the moonlight and he thought:

"I am sure my neighbor wouldn't mind if I took a few beans."

So he started to fill his hat with a few beans from the pile.

Grayeagle did not see the hoe his neighbor had left standing against the pile and, when he stepped on the blade, the handle came up and hit him on the nose.

"No! No!" Grayeagle shouted, "Here! I will pay you for the beans!"

You will probably notice that a Pima can laugh at himself. It is one way of seeing the other fellow's point of view. To us that is an important part of religion. The old people were well trained in this long ago. They could see the point of view even of their enemies, of all living things, especially animals.

There is a story about Big John that shows you what I mean:

One day, Big John was going along a trail that went past a big mesquite tree. Under the mesquite tree there was a coyote lying sleeping. Big John took off his hat and threw it at the coyote saying: "Wha-a-ah!!"

When the coyote jumped up the chin strap of the hat caught under his chin. Away went the coyote with the hat back of his ears.

Big John laughed so hard he said it was worth losing a hat for.

But the Pimas know that not everything about religion or life is humorous. There are other things.

One thing I am sure of. The smarter a man is the more he needs God to protect him from thinking he knows everything.

PIMA LEGENDS

AS handed down from our forefathers the Pima legends speak of the beginning of the earth, the creation, of the making of the animals, and the first men. One story tells about a great flood.

Some of these stories are very long. The one about White Clay Eater takes four nights to tell. Later I will tell a small part of this legend, but not all of it. I do not know it all. If I did, it would be a book by itself.

In many of the legends there are characters you would call earth spirits.

One of these spirits is 'Uam-ipudam, meaning Yellow Dress. She is a spirit of the desert who appears as a very appealing old woman who transforms scenes or objects into beauty. She appears mostly to children, leading them away, telling them of wonderful places that they will see if they go with her. She leads them on and on until they are far away from their homes. Then she disappears.

I know about 'Uam-ipudam personally. When I was very young another boy and myself were the victims of her bidding. We followed her many miles before my father, led by our tracks, found us and took us back home.

I know of one boy who went thirty-five miles to another village where he was found and taken back to his home. This boy is now an old man and has told me his story. He still dreams about the beautiful place shown to him by the strange old woman.

When I read in the paper about children getting lost in the desert I think that perhaps it was only the yellow blossoms of the Palo Verde that seemed to be 'Uam-ipudam calling them.

The word in the Pima language for "Something Told" is *ha'ichu'a·ga*. In the winter evenings while Rainbow's Ends was roasting corn over the fire, we would ask Keli·hi to tell us something. Sometimes he would tell us how to behave so that we would grow up to be good people, or he would tell us things that happened when his father Eaglefeathers was a boy. All these things are *ha'ichu'a·ga*. But so are legends, and those are what we liked most to hear.

LEGEND OF THE HUHUGAM

MANY, many years ago there came from the east a great army of tribes. This great army of tribes came conquering other people who lived along the way. On and on they came until they came to a valley. Here they found people living in villages with high adobe walls around them. In each of these villages lived a great chief with his people.

The first village they came to was near Blackwater. There, in a tall four-story adobe building lived a chief who was called Blue Hawk. The great army of tribes camped outside the walls of Blue Hawk's big house, and their chiefs met to plan how to conquer it.

They could not think of a way. So Old Man Coyote said that he would help them.

The first thing Old Man Coyote did was to put the Gophers to work boring holes under the adobe walls to weaken them. Then he put the Rats to work creeping into the homes of the warriors to chew their bow-strings so they could not be used. Then he sent the Owls out to set fire to anything that would burn.

Early in the morning he sent the Buzzards out to fly over Blue Hawk's big house to spy out its defenses.

When all the animals returned and reported, the great army of tribes attacked Blue Hawk's big house and conquered it.

On went the army of tribes conquering other walled villages. On they went toward the setting sun until they came to a boiling pot as big as a mountain.

As no one could get close enough to this pot to smash it, everyone was afraid. Everyone except Old Man Coyote. He held a war shield over his head and crept close to the great boiling pot and with a war club he smashed it.

When he returned to the chiefs of the army of tribes, Old Man Coyote asked them to honor him by saying: "Coyote did it!"

And so they did.

To please him, the chiefs shouted: "Coyote did it!"

Then on they went to the west until they came to an ocean, and there they met a great fish that no one could catch or kill.

Everyone who came near this fish was swallowed and disappeared, and everyone was afraid. Everyone except Old Man Coyote. He called the chiefs together and told them to permit the great fish to swallow them all, all at once.

And so they did. And after the fish had swallowed them they all stuck their spears into him and out through his sides and they killed him.

When the chiefs came out of the great dead fish, they all began to shout: "Coyote did it!"

But Old Man Coyote had disappeared. He had gone on to give his council to other people.

The great army of tribes could go no farther west because of the ocean. So they returned the way they had come.

When one tribe came to a place they had seen before and thought was a good place, there they settled. When another tribe came to a place they liked, that became their land, and there they stayed.

It was many years ago when all this happened.

The great boiling pot is still there broken to pieces. It was a volcano.

The great fish has long since been eaten up by other fish. It was a whale.

The great house of Blue Hawk is still there as the great army of tribes left it, in ruins. It is called Casa Grande.

The different tribes are still where they wanted to be, the Yumas near the Colorado River, the Papagos in their desert, and the Pimas in the Gila Valley.

And Old Man Coyote is around somewhere ready to give his council if you need him.

THE LEGEND OF HO'OK

 A LONG time ago there was an old woman whose name was Ho'ok, which means: "One Who Grabs." She was not well liked by the Pimas.

This ugly old woman lived in a cave where she could watch everything that went on in all the surrounding villages. When a new baby was born, she was sure to be the first to call at that home.

With devotional gestures and much emotion she would ask the mother the favor of holding the dear little baby in her arms. The mother was afraid not to, so she would hand over the baby, and Ho'ok would walk around with it for a while. Then all of a sudden she would run off with the baby.

This happened so many times that the people began to try to think of some way to get rid of such a nuisance.

At that time there lived in another cave in the South Mountains the little man who was called Se'ehe. This little man was gifted with the power to perform the impossible. So the people sent a messenger to see Se'ehe about Ho'ok.

When the messenger arrived at the cave of Se'ehe in the South Mountains he found the little man sound asleep. So he asked:

"Nab si ko·sh? Are you *sound* asleep?"

"No", said the little man. But he was. And he would not wake up, even when the messenger shook him.

In the center of Se'ehe's cave there had been a fire. The fire had burned down to ashes and live coals. The messenger picked up a hot live coal and dropped it on the chest of the little man. The coal burned down to ashes. Still the little man would not wake up. So the messenger placed all the live coals and the ashes on top of little Se'ehe who finally woke up and said:

"I-yah! Sha·chu pedr mos, i si n-kudrut.

Whose grandchild are you to bother me when I am sleeping so peacefully?"

The messenger excused himself and said that he was there on a mission for his people. He said that they wanted Se'ehe to stop old Ho'ok from running away with their babies.

When the little man heard what the messenger wanted he said:

"I beg your pardon.

You must be hungry after traveling so far.

Here is some pumpkin-pudding."

And he filled a very small cup full of pudding.

The messenger noticed how very small the cup was and wondered how it could be so small. But when he started to eat the pudding, he found that the little cup always stayed full. So he ate and ate until he had eaten as much as he could.

When he put the cup down, it was still full.

"What's the matter?" asked little Se'ehe, "Don't you like pudding?"

With one sweep of his finger, he cleaned out the whole contents of the cup.

Then the little man told the messenger what his people had to do to get rid of Ho'ok. Se'ehe said:

"Tell your people to gather wood and to make preparations for a big dance. In four days I will be there."

The messenger went back and told his people what they had to do. And they did what Se'ehe told them to do. They gathered wood, and they made preparations for a big dance. While they were doing this they met old Ho'ok and told her about the big dance in her honor and she said:

"*Chai! Mo·msi ganha wedr s-ho·ho'idam!*
Hey! Grandchildren, that is what I like!"

On the night of the fourth day when the big dance was to be held, little Se'ehe arrived at the village. Then he went over to the cave of Ho'ok. Personally he escorted her to the dance. When the people saw these two coming down the mountain they shouted:

"*Ho'ok-na! Ho'ok-na!*"

All of the men wanted to dance with Ho'ok, but little Se'ehe kept that honor to himself. He would not let anyone dance with her. Only he danced with Ho'ok until the singing stopped. Then everybody rested. Se'ehe and Ho'ok rested.

While they were resting the little man took out

his tobacco pouch and gave it to Ho'ok. She did not know that the tobacco was mixed with earth flowers. She smoked the tobacco mixed with earth flowers.

Then the singing started again and everyone began to dance.

As they danced faster and faster, the earth flowers began to make old Ho'ok sleepier and sleepier until at last she was so sleepy that her eyes began to close.

Then little Se'ehe told the singers to stop singing and the dancers to stop dancing. And they did. Everyone was silent. Some marched up to Ho'ok's cave and others lifted the sleeping old woman up onto little Se'ehe's back and he carried her up to her cave.

The men who had gone ahead had filled the cave of Ho'ok with wood. When Se'ehe came there he took his burden into the deepest corner of the cave and left the ugly old woman there. She was still sleeping. When the little man came out he set fire to the wood in the cave and it blazed up and filled the cave with flames.

The mountain trembled with the heat and roared and shook with the flames inside it and got so hot that it began to crack open all the way up to the top.

When the little man saw the mountain beginning to crack open he ran up on top and stamped his foot down on the crack and closed it.

And that was the end of Ho'ok.

When women are disagreeable they are called Ho'ok. She was not a pleasant person.

EAGLEMAN

A LONG time ago, there lived an Indian with his daughter. This beautiful girl was called Two Flowers. Every morning she would go down to the spring to get water. And every day a certain young man would meet her there and ask her to marry him.

The father of Two Flowers did not like this. So one day he gave the girl some *pinole* mixed with ground eagle feathers and told her to tell the boy that she would marry him if he would drink some of the *pinole.*

Two Flowers took the *pinole* and went down to the spring. There the young man came again and asked her to marry him. She said that she would like to and that she would if he would drink some of the *pinole.* The young man said that he would be glad to. So she mixed some of the *pinole* with water and gave it to him. He drank it and soon pimples began to come all over his body. He drank some more and feathers began to open out all over him. Soon he was covered with the feathers of an eagle!

Two Flowers saw this and ran home and told her father what had happened, and her father spread the word around the village. He took his bow and arrows and went out to the spring to see if what Two Flowers told him was true.

Sure enough, there sat the young man who had

become Eagleman. His body was covered all over with the feathers of an eagle. When the people came out to look at him, Eagleman started to fly away. As he circled around and around to gain height, the people shot arrows at him, but he grabbed the arrows in his claws. That is why there is an eagle on a silver dollar with a bunch of arrows in its claws.

When he had escaped from the people who shot arrows at him, Eagleman flew south until he came to a high peak. There he tried to light. But he only kicked the top of the peak off.

On he flew to the south until he came to another higher peak. On this peak, he rested. There he made his home. It was a lonely place where he lived.

The Pimas and Papagos call this mountain *Vavgiwulk,* which means "Cliff that is Small in the Middle." On the maps it is called Baboquivari.

One day Eagleman flew down from this mountain, back to the home of Two Flowers. He flew down past the people who had shot arrows at him, and picked up the girl who had given him the *pinole* to drink, and he carried her back to his nest on the mountain. There, he made her his mate, and there they lived together, and soon a little son was born to them.

Each day Eagleman flew down from his mountain to hunt game in the desert. Each day he would return to his nest and eat his food. Then he would go to sleep.

As often as he could find them, he would eat

the people who had shot arrows at him.

At last the people held a council to find out what could be done to destroy Eagleman, and someone suggested that they call on little Se'ehe.

They all agreed that calling on Se'ehe would be the best thing to do.

A messenger was sent to the South Mountains where the little man lived. On his way the messenger stopped at the house of Two Flowers' father and told him of his mission. The father of Two Flowers joined the messenger and on they went to Se'ehe's home.

When they found the little man they told him about the wishes of the people, and Se'ehe said:

"In four days I will come."

On the fourth day all the people went to the foot of the mountain *Vav-giwulk* to watch the rescue.

When Se'ehe arrived, he looked up at the mountain. Then he started to climb.

In some places the cliffs were straight up and down. But at last he reached the top where he found Two Flowers and her little son. Two Flowers was glad to see Se'ehe. She had hoped that some day he would come to rescue her.

Eagleman was away on a hunting trip, so the little man asked Two Flowers about her husband. She said that always after Eagleman returned from hunting and ate his lunch, he would take a nap.

"That is good," said Se'ehe. "I shall hide myself

and after he has eaten, you must encourage him to go to sleep. When he has fallen asleep, you must whistle as a signal for me to come out." Then Se'ehe changed himself into a fly and hid with the rest of the flies.

When he had become a fly he whispered to Two Flowers to ask if it was noticeable that he was not a fly? She said that it was not noticeable. So, there, among the other flies, little Se'ehe settled down and lay waiting.

Soon a deep roaring noise was heard as Eagleman came flying home. Also the people at the foot of the cliff could hear the low moaning of a man Eagleman was bringing home for his lunch. Se'ehe crawled down deeper among the other flies.

When Eagleman settled on top of the mountain and dropped his load, his little son ran out to meet him saying:

"*Apapa chu·wich.*" Over and over he said this.

"What does the child mean?" Eagleman asked his wife.

And she said: "He is trying to tell you that he is glad you have come home."

So Eagleman ate his lunch.

After he had eaten, he lay down to sleep. As soon as he was asleep, Two Flowers whistled the signal to Se'ehe. But Eagleman heard her and asked:

"Did you whistle?"

"Yes," she said, "I whistled because I was admiring your appetite."

102

So Eagleman went back to sleep. When he was sound asleep she gave the signal again. This time he did not waken. And this time little Se'ehe came out. He came out and picked up a big rock and smashed the head of Eagleman.

Then he carried Two Flowers and her little son down the steep cliff.

At the foot of the cliff the people watched. Among them was the father of Two Flowers. When she was safely on the ground he was surprised.

He did not know that he had a grandson. But he met them both with open arms and took them home.

No one knows much about this little man Se'ehe these days, but they used to say that he created the earth and everything on it. Nobody worshipped him. They only spoke of him as having strange powers. That seems to be true because, after he rescued Two Flowers from Eagleman and brought them down from the top of *Vav-giwulk,* the little man disappeared. No one has ever seen him after that time.

LEGEND OF THE GREAT FLOOD

A LONG time ago, there lived in these parts a tribe of Indians who hunted and fished and roamed all over these valleys.

One day it began to rain. It rained for days. It rained for weeks until the rivers began to rise with flood water. Soon the rivers over-flowed their banks and the people began to seek higher ground. The water kept coming up and up and up, and the people began to climb up and up and up to the highest mountain peaks. The water kept coming up until it covered all the valleys, until only the tops of the mountains could be seen. The people who climbed up on Superstition Mountain huddled together and watched the water coming up. With them there was a dog. One night the dog spoke in plain words: "The water has come."

Then the water came over the top of Superstition Mountain, drowning the people who were up there.

The water went on rising up and up and the birds flew up and up, until they reached the sky where they hung on by their bills. The water kept coming up until the woodpecker's tail was under water, and he began to cry. At his side a little sparrow was hanging by his bill, and the sparrow said to the woodpecker:

"You big cry baby!

Here I am just a little bird and I don't cry."

"Yes, but look at my tail! It's under water!" said the woodpecker.

"Well! Stop crying! You are only making matters worse with your tears! Adding to all this water.

Maybe if you stop crying the water will go down."

The woodpecker stopped crying and sure enough the water started going down. It went down and down and down until the tops of the mountain could be seen, and the little sparrow flew down, down to the earth again. And so did the woodpecker.

The next time you see a woodpecker, notice its tail. You can still see where it had been in the water many, many years ago.

And if you are ever southeast of Superstition Mountain, look to the top! You will see people still up there, turned into stone. Those are the people who were drowned during the flood.

How long ago did this happen? I cannot say, but this story was handed down to me by very old people.

LEGEND OF THE BIG DROUGHT

MANY years ago there came a time when no rains fell for many days. For many, many days, no rain fell at all until there was no grass on the desert and the creeks and water holes were dry.

High in the mountains lived Puma, Bear, and the other wild animals who depend on deer and antelope for their meat. The deer and antelope had left their running grounds in search of grass and drinking water, and Puma, Bear and the other wild animals could not find any game on their hunting trips. They were hungry.

So one night they held a council, and Puma said:

"Tomorrow morning!

You, Brown Buzzard, go to that highest peak over there and look around and see what you can find out."

Early the next morning Brown Buzzard went to the highest peak and there he sat all day. Late in the afternoon he noticed dust in the distance and watched as it drifted to a certain place and stopped. Brown Buzzard flew down from the mountain and went over to where the dust stopped. As he approached, a man said:

"Somebody is coming!"

Another man asked:

"What kind of clothes has he got on?"

The first man said:

"A brown suit, a red cap and spurs."

The other man said:

"Oh, he's alright. Just don't pay any attention to him. He's only a buzzard."

So Brown Buzzard sat down on the ground and watched as the men worked.

They were butchering deer and antelope. They had gathered all the game animals into a corral where they fed and watered them, and every so often they would go to the corral and butcher one of them for meat.

Brown Buzzard sat there watching until the men went away. Then he scooped up the blood of the butchered animals and took it home.

That evening Puma and Bear and the other wild animals held another council to hear what Brown Buzzard had found out.

Brown Buzzard said: "I found out something but the sun was so bright I did not see it very clear.

I suggest that Old Man Coyote go up on the high peak tomorrow and see what he can find out."

Brown Buzzard made this suggestion knowing that Old Man Coyote would do something mischievous.

And sure enough, when Old Man Coyote got up on the peak he began to sing. He scared all the deer and the antelope and they jumped out of the corral and scattered over the desert and the mountains.

Old Man Coyote sat on the mountain and sang and sang. After a while it began to rain and the water-holes filled up and the desert was soon covered with grass.

"See what I have done!" sang Old Man Coyote.

And Puma and Bear and the other hungry wild animals went out hunting again.

WHITE CLAY EATER

 NESTLED among the foothills of a very large mountain was a little valley. Starting somewhere upon the mountain a little brook flowed through this valley.

Along the banks of this little brook grew many trees that bore fruit and nuts in season. The birds and wild animals liked to come to this little valley to feed on the berries and grass that grew there. And when they had their fill, the animals would lie down in the shade of the trees to chew the cud and rest.

This little valley was the home of a very beautiful young woman named Twilight who lived there all alone.

One day when she went to swim in the brook and to listen to the singing birds, a voice called to her from among the trees. She went into the shadow of the trees to see who had called to her. In the shadow she saw a young man. He stood there without speaking. She did not know his name. Without speaking he made love to her and when he went away into the shadows she still did not know his name.

Until this time her name had been Twilight. But now she was called White Clay Eater because every day until her twin sons were born there was nothing she wanted to eat except white clay.

When her two boys were born she named them Sun and Moon.

These were the two children of White Clay Eater.

They grew up in the little valley where there were no other people. They knew how to find wild fruit for food and they became good hunters, killing only game they needed for meat.

When these two strong young men grew old enough to have wives, their mother began to make a plan.

There were no other people in the little valley, but not very far away up the river there lived a man named Wyhum-newhe who had two beautiful daughters.

It was the plan of White Clay Eater to call these two beautiful girls into her valley so that her sons could take them to be their wives.

So she called to her boys and said:

"Moon! Sun! Toward the southwest near the east end of the mountain two days and one night away there is a swampy place where bamboos grow. I want you to go to that place and cut two pieces of bamboo and bring them back to me."

As their mother told them to do, the two boys went out two days and one night away to the swampy place and cut two pieces of bamboo and brought them back to her.

For two days and one night White Clay Eater worked on the pieces of bamboo carving them into flutes. And when the flutes were finished she called to her boys and said:

"Sun! Moon! Now I will teach you a certain

tune that must be played on these flutes exactly as I teach it to you."

And she taught them a certain tune that was very beautiful.

Then she said: "I would like to hear how your music sounds from a distance. So go out across the valley and stand on that big rock over there and play."

Moon and Sun took their flutes and went out across the valley and stood on the big rock and played the music their mother had taught them.

White Clay Eater knew that always on this day of the year the two beautiful daughters of Wyhum-newhe came to bathe in a spring near the big rock. She also knew that the names of these girls were Morning Star and Evening Star.

As Moon and Sun played on their flutes, White Clay Eater listened and knew that her plan would succeed, so sweetly over the air came the tune she had taught them.

The two beautiful daughters of Wyhum-newhe were in the spring bathing when the music went out everywhere into the air.

Evening Star had gone into the water first and as her ears touched the surface of the water she heard the music! It came from the east. She listened for a while and then she said:

"Oh sister! Hurry and come into the water! I hear music coming over the air from somewhere!"

Morning Star got into the water and listened toward the east and toward the west. Then she said:

"I don't hear anything."

Evening Star said:

"Put your ears down to the surface of the water!"

Morning Star did, and she heard the sweet music coming from the west.

She listened for a while and then said:

"We must go now and see who is making such beautiful music!"

So they got out of the water and ran to their home and began to get ready to go away.

"I know where you are going," said their father. "You are going to look for the music makers."

The girls did not have time to answer him. They went away to look for whoever it was that made such beautiful music.

After traveling for some distance, first to the east and then to the west, they came to a small house and a little man with a long nose met them at the door, and Morning Star asked:

"Do you know who makes that good music?"

The little man with a long nose said:

"Of course I know because I am the one who makes that music."

And Evening Star said:

"All right then, play us a tune so that we may know you are the one!"

The little man went to a dry old tree near his house and climbed up to the top of the tree and began pecking at it and making a funny little rattling noise.

Then he came down out of the tree, and Morning Star asked: "Is that all?"

The little man said:

"Early in the morning I sing that way and everybody seems to like it."

The girls told him they were sorry but that was not the music they were looking for, and they left the little man and went on their way.

After they were out of sight the little man slapped himself on the side of his head and said:

"What a fool I have made of myself!

I could have told them I know where that music is coming from! I could have told them where Sun and Moon live! Now those girls will tell everyone what a fool I am and everybody will laugh at me!"

Morning Star and Evening Star went on until they came to another house where they were met by a man with a big round head and big round eyes who asked them: "Who do you want to see?"

The girls said:

"We want to see who makes the most beautiful music we have ever heard. Do you know who it is?"

"Certainly I know because I am the one who makes that music."

And the girls asked:

113

"Will you play us a tune so we may know that you are the one?"

The man with a big round head and big round eyes went over to a cottonwood tree near his house and settled himself on one of the highest branches and began to hoot.

After hooting for a while he came down, and Evening Star asked: "Is that all?"

"Yes," said Owl, "That is all. Early in the morning before the sun is up I hoot and people for miles around seem to enjoy it. It doesn't sound so good this late with the sun shining, does it?"

The girls said: "No."

They said it was not the music they were looking for, and they went on.

After they had gone, Owl said:

"I am a hog!

Wanting to hog the glory I don't deserve! I could have told them I know where that music is coming from! I could have easily directed them to the house of Moon and Sun.

I enjoy hearing that music myself every morning after I have stopped hooting. What's the matter with me!

People used to call me a wise old owl. Now they can call me pig!

They were·such nice looking girls, too!"

He hit himself on the side of the head and said:

"Me and my big mouth!"

Morning Star and Evening Star went on and on. They went first to the north and then to the south.

At last they came to a little valley nestled among the foothills of a large mountain where a little brook flowed and birds sang in the trees and wild animals fed on the grass.

In front of a small house a woman sat weaving a basket. She said to the girls:

"I have been waiting for you for a long time."

It was White Clay Eater.

Over the air from the big rock beside the spring came the music of the flutes of Sun and Moon playing the tune their mother had taught them to play.

Morning Star and Evening Star listened to the music and they knew at last who was making the music that led them away from the home of their father, Wyhum-newhe.

And so Moon and Evening Star were married, and Sun and Morning Star were married, and they all lived happily ever after.

THE LEGEND OF TODAY

THE legends I have told were told by the old Pimas many, many years ago to entertain and instruct their children. Today, these old stories are almost forgotten by the younger Pimas.

I don't think they should be forgotten. They are a part of Pima tradition. They show what life was like in those old days and what bothered people such as floods and drought and old Ho'ok's bad manners. They show what our ancestors thought was important. They help us to understand what is important today.

Sometimes I think what is happening to the Pima Indians today is a legend, only it is harder to believe.

As you know, this writing began before the coming of the white man. It told about events in the times of Eaglefeathers, and Keli•hi, and in the days of my own boyhood. It showed how many things were changed, but how the Pimas went on working happily on their farms with plenty of water and good harvests.

For many years the old Pima way of life went on the same. The people put on clothes and hats, built adobe houses, learned English, and bought groceries in a grocery store. They had wagons and horses and became Christians, and went hunting with rifles instead of bows and arrows. All these things were unimportant because they still farmed and brought in good harvests.

My own life is still a good life. My children are all married and settled down. I have a number of grandchildren. From my porch I can look out at the mountains I have been looking at all my life. I have nothing to complain of personally.

Sometimes I go over to the town of Chandler and play checkers or shuffleboard with some other retired gentlemen from the east. I haven't been over much of late since I have been busy with this writing. Often I sit looking out at those mountains that are always the same although they seem to change when the light changes. I think about my old people who are gone, and the ancient Huhugam who lived near those mountains hundreds of years before the time of Eaglefeathers. I think about how long a time the Pima Indians have lived by farming.

I don't farm any more myself, but some of my boys work some good land not far away towards those mountains. They are fortunate, because not every Pima has enough water to farm.

Today the Pima Indian is doing his best to get along under the white man's conditions, striving to make a living any way he can. He may live in a good home, drive a nice car, and can go into a bar when he wants to have a drink.

Like the white man, he can drink too much and run into an accident on the highway and get himself killed. Like the white man, he sometimes has to worry about the money to make a payment on his television set. Sometimes he plays around and his home life is broken up. Yes, the Pima Indian is getting civilized.

I know he has to learn the white man's way or be left behind. But not everything he is learning is good.

When somebody asks me: "How would you rather live, the old Indian way or the white way?" I say: "The old Indian way." I think how I would like to go hunting again with a bow and arrow in New York Thicket, or go fishing and swim in a river running full of water!

I say this, but I don't believe I would say it except for the Pima Indian's two problems of land and water.

The Pima legend of today is about land and water. I will now tell that story.

LAND

NOT long ago, a car stopped in front of our house and four men got out and came up on the porch. As I met them they asked:

"Do you own this land?"

I said I did.

"How much land do you have?"

I said: "Thirty acres."

"Do you want to sell it?"

I said that I did not have the deed to it.

"Where is the deed?"

"At the Agency."

They said: "If you agree to sell, we can get the deed from the Agency."

"What do you offer? It is good land with plenty of water."

"Four hundred dollars an acre. Twelve thousand dollars for the thirty."

I asked: "Have you talked to the Agency?"

They said: "We have."

I said: "I am sorry but this place is not for sale!"

They left. I wasn't interested. But it set me to wondering.

I was glad they came to me and not to some other Indians I know because some of them would take an offer for less.

119

These same people who wanted my land bought some other land nearby, not on the Reservation, for which, I am told, they paid $600.00 an acre.

I am telling about these offers to familiarize you with the value of our land on this Reservation. The land that has water. I am wondering what the Pima tribe would soon be like if we were allowed to sell. My hope is that the government will never give us our deeds. If an Indian sells his land there would soon be just another case for relief.

I know that some Pimas are trying to sell their land now. The only thing that is protecting them is the government holding their deeds, keeping the Reservation together. The State would like to have all restrictions removed so they can tax the Reservation land.

Some of our white neighbors seem to think that our farms ought to be taxed the same as theirs. But so far as I remember we have never received any payment for some good land which is no longer ours.

WATER

IN THE old days, all the Pima Indians made a good living working their farms which produced a good yield. There was plenty of feed and water along the Gila River for their stock. Many lived in nice adobe homes of which a few are still in use today.

They maintained their own water system, distributing the water to anyone needing it the most. When a dam washed out by flood water, they all went out and put in another brush dam. When an irrigation ditch needed cleaning, they went out together with their shovels and cleaned it out.

There were only a few farm machines, but they had the plow, drawn by horses. Even plowing was done from farm to farm by someone who had a plow and a team. At other times the people he plowed for did something for him. Every field was put into crop. And so successful was their planting that if you climbed to the top of one of the nearby hills, as far as your eyes could see, you would see green along the river. All this was the result of helping each other, and having plenty of water from the Gila River. That is how the Pimas farmed in the Gila Valley for hundreds of years.

Then came a time when all this was changed.

A dam was put across the Gila River, upstream from the Pimas.

The purpose of this dam was to hold the waters of the rainy season and let it out for irrigation use in the dry times.

It took a long time for that dam to fill up and when it did, the water no longer came down the Gila. The Pimas were left without any water at all, to irrigate their farms or water their stock or even to drink. They dug wells. The wells dried up. The stock began to die. The sun burned up the farms. Where everything used to be green, there were acres of desert, miles of dust, and the Pima Indians were suddenly desperately poor.

They had never worked for wages. They chose to stay on the Reservation. It was their home.

That was a time before electricity and gas were much in use, so the demand for wood was large. There was plenty of wood on the Reservation, so the Pimas became sellers of wood. The price for wood was small, but wood saved them from starving. Today there are no mesquite trees left on the Reservation that are not second growth. If you look at the base of any mesquite tree you will find a dry stump. That is where a much bigger tree once grew.

For many years the Pimas lived somehow without farming. They still had their land, but no water. It was hard. But harder when white people used to accuse us of being lazy for not working our farms.

The Pimas didn't say much about their trouble. But finally some white missionaries and other friends of the Indians spoke to someone in the Government.

What came of this was the San Carlos Dam, later called Coolidge Dam. This dam was built up in a canyon of the Gila River, and its purpose was to conserve water especially for the use of the Pima Indians.

The Pima lands, after lying idle for so many years, had been covered with brush and mesquite, so the Government came in with heavy equipment and cleared and leveled about fifty thousand acres on the Reservation. These lands were made ready for the flow of irrigation water, and the people were happy, thinking that now they would be able to farm again.

This is not all the Government did for the Pimas, they issued to them an assortment of farm machinery. Many Indians, who did not have any implements left, took advantage of this and equipped their farms with mowers, racks, wagons and teams to pull them. Some of these people are still paying for that equipment today. The issue was of course reimbursable. But at that time the Pimas were happy and confident. When the dam was completed there would be plenty of water.

And there was. For about five years. Then the water began to run short again. After another five years it stopped altogether.

What happened?

Some speculators had bought up desert land under this dam and sold it with water rights. They sold the land fast and they sold a lot of it. The irrigation water didn't go far, so the farmers began to drill wells. They drilled so many wells and ran so many hundreds of pumps day and night that the water table sank almost out of reach and they began to fight each other for the underground water.

On the Reservation the Pimas had about a dozen wells, and the white farmers criticized us for taking away their underground flow.

You can guess how much water ever got to the Reservation, and what the Pima farms began to look like.

In the old days, on hot summer nights, a low mist would spread over the river and the sloughs. Then the sun would come up and the mist would disappear. On those hot nights the cattle often gathered along the river up to their knees in the cool mud.

Soon some Pima boy would come along and dive into the big ditch and swim for awhile. Then he would get out and open the headgate and the water would come splashing into the laterals and flow out along the ditches. By this time all the Pimas were out in the fields with their shovels. They would fan out and lead the water to the alfalfa, along the corn rows, and over to the melons. The red-wing blackbirds would sing in the trees and fly down to look for bugs along the ditches. Their song always means that there is water close by as they will not sing if there is not water splashing somewhere.

The green of those Pima fields spread along the river for many miles in the old days when there was plenty of water.

Now the river is an empty bed full of sand.

Now you can stand in that same place and see the wind tearing pieces of bark off the cottonwood trees along the dry ditches.

The dead trees stand there like white bones. The red-wing blackbirds have gone somewhere else. Mesquite and brush and tumbleweeds have begun to turn those Pima fields back into desert.

Now you can look out across the valley and see the green alfalfa and cotton spreading for miles on the farms of white people who irrigate their land with hundreds of pumps running night and day. Some of those farms take their water from big ditches dug hundreds of years ago by Pimas, or the ancestors of Pimas. Over there across the valley is where the red-wing blackbirds are singing today.

I am not criticizing our Government, or most of the men who administer its program. Only one or two who shut their eyes to justice when the pressure gets too much on them.

There are some very smart white operators coming into this desert country these days with money and influence. Not all of them can write their name. They have a string of lawyers to do that for them.

I had two years in business school, but only last year I let a white man take me on a business deal for two thousand dollars.

And he had never even been to High School.

The Pimas are a very humble people who like to farm. Perhaps they have been too humble. They are intelligent in their own way, and many of them have had a good education. But the pace of progress is a little hard on them. I have heard several white men say that the pace of what is called progress today is almost too much for *them*.

Think how it must seem to a simple Pima who remembers the Gila River when it was a running stream.